THE WORLD'S BEST
BARTENDERS' GUIDE

THE WORLD'S BEST
BARTENDERS' GUIDE

PROFESSIONAL BARTENDERS FROM THE

WORLD'S GREATEST BARS TEACH YOU

HOW TO MIX THE PERFECT DRINK

Joseph Scott and Donald Bain

HPBooks
A STONESONG PRESS BOOK

HPBooks
Published by The Berkley Publishing Group
A member of Penguin Putnam Inc.
375 Hudson Street
New York, New York 10014

A Stonesong Press Book
Copyright © 1998 by Stonesong Press and
Joseph Scott and Donald Bain
Book design by Richard Oriolo
Cover design by Joe Lanni
Cover photograph © Jonnie Miles/Photonica

First edition: November 1998

Published simultaneously in Canada.

The Penguin Putnam Inc. World Wide Web site address is
http://www.penguinputnam.com

Library of Congress Cataloging-in-Publication Data

Scott, Joseph, 1945-
    The world's best bartenders' guide : professional
bartenders from the world's greatest bars teach you
how to mix the perfect drink / Joseph Scott and Donald
Bain. — 1st ed.
        p.   cm.
    Includes index.
    ISBN 1-55788-296-7
    1. Bartending.   2. Cocktails.   3. Bars, (Drinking
establishments)   I. Bain, Donald, 1935-
II. Title.
TX951.S4255   1998
641.8'74—dc21   98-30033
                                                            CIP

Printed in the United States of America

10   9   8   7   6   5   4   3   2   1

FOR RENÉE AND LADY P

CONTENTS

PREFACE

Tastemakers are increasingly forgoing the tame offerings
of the microbrewery and the vine in favor of high-octane
cocktails.
Vanity Fair, July 1996

Entertaining at home makes many demands upon a host and hostess. Preparation of a festive meal can take days, and often does. But too many otherwise excellent hosts approach the predinner cocktail hour with a back-of-the-hand philosophy: Pour some liquor into a glass, add ice and a mixer, and hand it to guests. This is unfortunate because the preparation of drinks sets the tone for the entire afternoon or evening. How skillfully drinks are made, and presented, says a great deal about the host's erudition, image, and commitment to upscale entertaining—good friends, good talk, and good drinks.

TODAY'S TRENDS

It wasn't long ago that restaurant patrons headed straight for their tables. Today, there's a growing tendency to linger first at handsomely appointed bars manned by skilled, friendly, professional bartenders whose creativity with cocktails and mixed drinks rivals what the finest chefs are doing back in the kitchen.

Marie Maher, bartender at New York's Windows on the World, not only has developed a wide variety of signature drinks, but also has nurtured a steady clientele who take their drinks there because of her expertise and personality. She sums up the change in attitudes toward drinking with, "The age of the highball or the shot with a beer has definitely segued into the age of "up-cocktailism."

That's why we've reached out around the globe for advice from Marie Maher and others of the world's best professional bartenders. By heeding what these experts have to say, everyone hosting a party at home can pour the perfect drink, and present it the way the pros do every night.

PROFESSIONAL BARTENDERS

Professional bartenders are a prideful lot, which they should be. The good ones, and we've included only the good ones, juggle many skills as they strive to satisfy their diverse and often demanding customers. There's a portion of their brains in which is stored not only hundreds of drink recipes, many of them impossibly obscure, but also the drink preferences of their regular customers. On top of that, they're called upon to be pleasant, witty, and wise and, in general, to be the perfect hosts and hostesses at their respective bars—not an easy task. Those included in this book have mastered these demands, and more. They're professionals, and you will be, too, by following their advice.

THE WORLD'S GREATEST BARS

A word about how we chose these bars as the "world's greatest." Obviously, it had to be an arbitrary process. There are thousands of wonderful bars around the world, ranging from a popular neighborhood saloon to an elegant room high atop a downtown building, where the views match the perfectly concocted cocktail. We approached building the list in three ways.

First, we drew upon our personal experiences, comparing notes on where we've enjoyed excellent drinks prepared by skilled professionals. We've both traveled extensively and have enjoyed these experiences worldwide.

Then we called upon friends in various cities, who conducted Zagatlike informal polls of their friends and professional colleagues. When a particular bar was mentioned as one of that city's best by a majority of those polled, it became a serious contender.

And third, we were determined to achieve geographic diversity. The fifty greatest bars could easily have been developed from within one city—New York, San Francisco, Paris, or London. But there are great bars everywhere, in cities large and small and in every nation of the world. Eventually, we culled our choices from a much longer list of candidates. We're proud of our picks, stand behind them, and invite you, the readers, to submit your own candidates for future editions.

THE BOOK'S APPROACH

The structure of this book is different from that of any other bartenders' guide. To begin with, its direction has been dictated, to a great extent, by the input of our professional bartenders. We provided them with a long and detailed questionnaire, which established a platform from which to offer their advice and wisdom. In a sense, the questionnaire functioned as a poll; the results are sprinkled throughout the book in appropriate places, along with expert instruction on how to make the most popular drinks, and some that aren't so popular.

We also decided that other home bartender guides put too much emphasis on exotic drinks that few people will ever bother to make. We've included many of them, of course, but focus more on those drinks people actually do concoct, and consume.

The World's Best Bartenders' Guide represents yet another departure from other such books on the market. It doesn't make any sense to us for a reader who wishes to make a Martini to first have to go to a chapter on "Gin" and then seek out Martini recipes within that chapter. We've focused on the most popular drinks and have devoted sections to each. Once we've covered these popular libations, we go on to offer recipes for drinks requested less often.

Because our bartender sources represent a wide geographic spread, readers will be able to easily identify and to make drinks from a specific area of the country, or world, when entertaining guests from those places.

Alcoholic beverages, their origins, and historic uses have spawned many wonderful tales—some true, some apocryphal. We've offered a smattering of them throughout the book to give you, the home bartender, some intriguing knowledge that you can serve up to your guests along with the drinks.

What we hope to have created in this book is a valuable primer for making the perfect drink, and we also hope to have fostered an appreciation of approaching bartending in a professional manner. At the same time, the book functions as a mini travel guide, pointing you in the direction of bars we feel are *the best in the world.*

COCKTAILS VERSUS MIXED DRINKS

Before we proceed to the first chapter, which identifies our professional bartenders and describes the wonderful places in which they ply their trade, we wish to clarify whether this book is about cocktails or mixed drinks. There's a difference. *The World's Best Bartenders' Guide* is about both, although the emphasis is certainly on the cocktail.

Generally, the term *mixed drink* denotes the combining of an alcoholic beverage with a mixer and serving it over ice: Scotch and Soda, Gin and Tonic, Rum and Coke. Pretty simple, provided you adhere to the proper ratio of spirit to mixer (generally one part alcohol to eight parts mixer) and serve top-shelf liquor.

The *cocktail* is a more elaborate, subtle, and demanding challenge, ranging from the elegant, bone-dry Martini to the fanciest tropical drink, loaded with a blend of dark and light rums and topped with fruits of every variety.

A professionally created cocktail not only contains the right ingredients in the proper ratio but also creates a sense of anticipation. Mixed perfectly, adorned properly, and presented with flair, the cocktail can set an entire evening's tone, an afternoon's ambiance, or the mood of a late morning's brunch. Mixing a cocktail is both art and science as well as fun.

What we've set out to do in this book is to turn the reader into a confident, relaxed, and creative home bartender. If, after using it as your guide, you have pleased your guests with your bar and bartending skills, we'll have succeeded in that goal.

Our participating professional bartenders were asked many questions by the authors, including what special advice they might have for fledgling home bartenders. Their answers were many and varied, but we especially like the one given by Caroline Dohamel, bartender at Montreal's Sir Winston Churchill Pub: "Purchase yourself a good bartender's guide." Since you already have, you're on your way.

Happy reading, and mixing.

ACKNOWLEDGMENTS

Any book of this sort depends upon the input of many people. The professional bartenders and managers/owners of our fifty great participating bars head the list of those we wish to thank. But there are many other individuals who heard our call for help and rose to the occasion:

Dr. E. Z. Filler (a dentist, of course); Gary Kraut, who travels to places we've never heard of; Sanford Teller, quick and bright; Paul Fargis, president and publisher of The Stonesong Press, who thought the world needed a better bartender's guide; Bruce and Joane Filler-Varty, our tasteful Seattle consultants; Bill Wooby, connoisseur of Washington, DC's finer things; Laurie Bain Wilson, *Bridal Guide* magazine's crack travel editor; Sally Bulloch, executive manager of London's superb Athenaeum Hotel and Apartments; Allen J. Bernstein, whose Morton's Restaurants define "upscale"; John Duff, publisher of Perigee Books; Jeanette Egan, editor who made sure the book was as great as the bars and bartenders; Bill Littlefield and

Karen Marshall; Josh and Kelly Raphaelson; Tony Tedeschi, our eyes and ears in the Caribbean; Matt Miller, president of AICP and someone who knows what a good bar should be; Jim Grau; Joseph Baum, New York's premier restaurateur; Donna Filler-Wilensky, who knows Atlanta; San Francisco's Compass Rose Bar and Westin St. Francis Hotel's eloquent spokespeople, Marsha Monro and Lisa Pulice; Susan and Alan Schoenbach, and Juan Félix García for their hard work and dedication to bringing the Mojito and La Bodeguita del Medio to their rightful place on these pages; James Brady for directing us down Further Lane to the Blue Parrot; Theresa Delaney for pulling together details from Texas to London; Randy Beier of *Aspen Magazine* for introducing us to Grayson Stover; Bill Sertl of *Saveur* magazine and Gene Bourg of the New Orleans *Times Picayune*; Maebeth Fenton for all her help from Kennedy's to Mahon's and a fair few in between; Jim Kiewel, Robin Lampert, and Gina Grandinetti for their guidance in the Windy City; Jonathan Kiewel for his advice from New Orleans on up to Portland; Sian Griffiths in Hong Kong; Richard Fannon and Robin Hutson in Winchester, England; Bill Flanagan, who hangs out in Wollensky's but loves to recommend the Hemingway Bar at The Ritz; Sean Carberry, Ireland's foremost publicist, for getting us close enough to the Horseshoe Bar to score; Andre Moraillon for his insight into Paris; food and wine writer James Villas for his research help and his affirmation of The Pump Room; restaurant critic Bob Lape for his insight on single malts; Richard Vine, Ph.D., for his boundless knowledge of wines; and Gareth Edmonson-Jones for getting us high (38,000 feet).

THE WORLD'S FIFTY GREATEST BARS AND THEIR BARTENDERS*

As with life itself, things change—including bartenders. While most bartenders represented in the book have been at their posts for many years and are likely to remain there, an occasional defection is always possible. But the standards of each of the bars on the list of the world's greatest are sufficiently high to ensure that any replacement bartender will be top-notch.

It should also be noted that all the bars in the book serve food, or are associated with fine restaurants. But since this is a book about bartending, we've elected not to discuss food.

Some of the bartenders are also beverage directors of their establishments. We haven't tried to differentiate between these positions and trust that those who've risen to the management level will understand our need to focus on their bartending expertise.

*The bars are listed alphabetically by country and not in order of author preference.

CANADA

Montreal

737 RESTAURANT, CLUB AND LOUNGE
1 Place Ville-Marie, Bureau 1532
Montreal, Quebec
H3B 2B5, Canada
514-397-0737
Bartender: **PIERRE BEAUNOYER**

Known to loyal regulars as Altitude 737 because of its location atop one of the city's tallest buildings, this remarkable complex offers limitless views, superb drinks, and a chance to join what sometimes seems to be the entire population of Montreal enjoying themselves after work. It's the archetypical jet-set bar, disco, and restaurant, with consummate pros behind its multiple bars.

SIR WINSTON CHURCHILL PUB
1455-59 Crescent
Montreal, Quebec
H3G 2B2, Canada
514-288-3814
Bartender: **CAROLINE DOHAMEL**

Affectionately know by locals as "Winnie's," this bustling pub with seventeen (count 'em) bars has long been a favorite of such TV luminaries as David Letterman, who often mentions it on his show. Located on busy Crescent Street in romantic Montreal, it packs them in day and night, and for good reason. The staff is unfailingly pleasant, the drinks big and expertly mixed, and people-watching from two second-floor terraces is great entertainment.

Toronto

CLUB LUCKY
117 John Street
Toronto, Ontario
M5V 2E2, Canada
416-977-8890
Bartender: **LIZ CAPE**

Club Lucky typifies the burgeoning number of upscale, sophisticated bars featuring Martinis, now that they've burst back into vogue. That's good news for Toronto Martini lovers because Club Lucky offers a wide variety of them, some remarkably inventive—although Liz Cape winces when she recalls a customer asking for a "Tequilatini," a Martini made with tequila.

CHINA

Hong Kong

THE LOBBY AND BAR AT THE PENINSULA HOTEL
Salisbury Road
Kowloon, Hong Kong
852-2366-6251
Bartender: JOHNNY CHUNG

This is elegance refined to perfection. If the freedom to congregate and see and be seen in The Lobby and Bar at The Peninsula is ever mitigated, China will have more on its hands than an uprising. Had Hong Kong stayed within the Crown, Johnny Chung would likely have become Sir John. Regardless of politics, his cocktails and hospitality remain royal after thirty years—and timelessly welcome.

CUBA

Havana

LA BODEGUITA DEL MEDIO
Calle Emperado No. 207 b, Cuba and San Ignacio
La Habana Vieja, Havana City, Cuba
011-53-761-8442
Bartender: JORGE LORENZO VIQUEIRA LEE

You may not, at present, be able to sidle up to the bar at La Bodeguita and say, as Ernest Hemingway often did, "Let me have a Mojito." But start practicing, because who knows? We love this place, not just because it has one of the most colorful histories of any bar on the planet, but because its recipe book features drinks—starting with its own creation, the Mojito—*before* it gets to its outrageous Cuban cuisine.

DOMINICAN REPUBLIC

Puerto Plata

EXTASIS BAR, SINNER'S BAR AND POOL BAR
AMHSA Paradise Beach Club & Casino
Playa Dorada, Puerto Plata, Dominican Republic
800-752-9236
Bartender: LUCIANO "MAGIC" PILAR

Award-winning barman Luciano "Magic" Pilar offers what he terms his *real* professional bartending secret: "Make and serve every drink with love." Guests at this spectacular all-inclusive resort on the north coast of the Dominican Republic evidently appreciate Luciano's approach—he consistently wins the monthly hospitality award. The resort features 436 guest rooms and suites, three excellent restaurants, a disco, a casino and, of course, a staggering array of tropical drinks, many created by Luciano himself, whose recipes he shares with us in this book. His original drinks have garnered him numerous bartending awards, and he's vice president of the Dominican Bartender Association. Your guests will appreciate his "magic" when you serve them some of Magic's drinks on a hot summer afternoon on your patio.

ENGLAND

London

THE LIBRARY BAR AT THE LANESBOROUGH HOTEL
Hyde Park Corner
London SW12T4, England
011-44-171-259-5599 or 800-999-1828
Bartender: SALVATORE CALABRESE

The Library Bar at The Lanesborough Hotel elevated itself from good to great in 1995 with the hiring of barman Salvatore Calabrese, perhaps the world's foremost authority on antique Cognacs, Armagnacs, and Ports. Dukes Hotel's loss was the Lanesborough's gain, as this histrionic historian of spirits removes the corks from centuries-old bottles and sells their contents for hundreds of dollars a glass, all with a flair and, of course, a history lesson. Some of his recipes also appear in Salvatore's own book, *Classic Cocktails.*

THE WHISKY BAR AT THE ATHENAEUM HOTEL AND APARTMENTS
116 Piccadilly
London W1V OBJ, England
0171-499-3464
Bartender: **ROBERTO TONDO**

This handsomely paneled club room within the exquisite Athenaeum Hotel serves up seventy varieties of single-malt Scotch, and barman Roberto Tondo can explain their subtle differences. You might find yourself comparing the relative virtues of these splendid whiskys (there's never an "e" in *whisky* when it relates to Scotch) with today's hottest movie star, leading politico, or titan of global industry. Linger long enough and you'll be toasted by The Athenaeum's executive manager and one of London's hospitality industry's leading lights, Sally Bulloch, for whom the hotel's restaurant is named.

Winchester

HOTEL DU VIN & BISTRO
Southgate Street
Winchester, Hampshire SO23 9EF, England
011-44-196-284-1414
Bartender: **ROB ASHFIELD**

We witnessed Robin Hutson take a fifteen-pound rainbow trout from the nearby River Test during his first day ever fly-fishing, so it comes as no surprise that in a matter of three years he has created (with a great deal of help, he'll readily admit) one of the finest small hotels, restaurants, and bars in all of merry England. Each room at the inn is named after a famous vineyard, which gave barman Rob Ashfield a tough act to follow. Is it possible for a bartender to upstage the house?

Yes! (Now, if only Robin would share the credit with those who helped him catch that rainbow trout . . .)

FRANCE

Paris

THE CHINA CLUB
50, Rue de Charenton
75012 Paris, France
43-438202
Bartender: JUSTIN BARBEY

We've never met a writer who was a good professional bartender, but when we came across Justin Barbey, we found a professional bartender who is a good writer, even in his second language. Barman Justin explains: "If you can imagine a Parisian cocktail bar 'à la Chinoise' in all its glory—shakers rattling, elegant ladies and affluent gentlemen poised on the edge of their chairs, the reflection of candles in the lacquer work of the polished pillars, and the strains of Armstrong and Sinatra above the clatter of the restaurant cutlery—then you have a taste of the China Club. Add to this image that of a fellow, small in stature, gray-haired, simply dressed, and clutching two large plastic bags. Nobody, except for the staff, knows him. Nor would they guess the significance of the bags, with their freshly cut tomatoes, zucchinis, and cucumbers and the other vegetables and herbs. For a good Daiquiri, he'll pay four tomatoes and a couple of blue potatoes. For a bunch of thyme, we are talking a Whiskey Sour with Maker's Mark. Pumpkins and zucchinis will have him singing all the way home, and us stocked up with vegetables for the week." Now here's a man who should be writing his own bartender's guide!

HEMINGWAY BAR, THE HOTEL RITZ
Place Vendome
75001 Paris, France
43-163296
Bartender: COLIN FIELD

The Hotel Ritz, Paris, needs no more introduction than its name, which has passed the lips of royalty, world leaders, tycoons, movie stars, and rapscallions alike. But it wasn't until William Flanagan, editor, author, and bon vivant extraordinaire, spoke the words in context with the Hemingway Bar and Colin Field (in the very presence of Patrick Ford!) that we realized just how impressive The Ritz was within even our limited field of vision. Thank you, Bill; thank you, Colin; thank you, Papa.

GRENADA

St. Georges

SPICERS BAR, REX GRENADIAN HOTEL
Point Salines
St. Georges, Grenada
809-444-3333
Bartender: NEIL FELIX

Barman Neil Felix represented Grenada in the 1997 Caribbean Battle of the Bartenders, and won. Small wonder. In this tropical island paradise where nutmeg and cinnamon permeate the air, he serves up a dazzling array of tropical drinks, many of them of his own creation. Fortunately for the readers and users of this book, he was willing to share his most secret recipes, enabling every home bartender to bring a bit of Grenada into the home. But if you want steel drums, you're on your own.

IRELAND AND NORTHERN IRELAND

Dublin

THE HORSESHOE BAR, THE SHELBOURNE HOTEL
27 St. Stephen's Green
Dublin 2, Ireland
353-1-676-6471
Bartender: SEAN BOYD

The Shelbourne is easy to find; it is, according to lore, the most distinguished address in Ireland. Perhaps the most appealing reason for such notoriety is its Horseshoe Bar. What The Algonquin was to New York, what Raffles was to Singapore, The Shelbourne, and particularly its Horseshoe Bar, is to Dublin. It lured Thackeray, George Moore, and Elizabeth Bowen in this century, and more recently Bowen's chronicler, Derek Mahon, whose article on novelist Bowen and The Shelbourne, written for *Ireland of the Welcomes* magazine, was reprinted and used as a promotional brochure. We bow humbly before such literary roots but, nonetheless, plant our own little Horseshoe Bar seed herewith.

Irvinestone

MAHON'S PUB
Mill Street
Irvinestone, County Fermanagh
BT94 1GS, Northern Ireland
011-44-13656-21656
Bartender: JOE MAHON

Mahon's Pub is a cozy bar in a comfy little hotel of the same name in a sedate little village called Irvinestone. Irvinestone is in Northern Ireland, though this wee hamlet of 2,500 Protestants and Catholics has never itself been troubled during the decades of strife that have pitted neighbor against neighbor. The residents of Irvinestone, you see, back in 1908 set up a community group called The Trustees, the composition of which reflected the religious affiliations of the community, with the chair rotating between the different groups. As a result, Irvinestone has never had any violence or sectarianism. And Mahon's is a very friendly pub, owner-operated for three generations by Joe Mahon, Joe Mahon, Jr., and Joe Mahon III, all of whom were born in the place. "Up there in Room 4," Joe will tell you, as he points with his thumb over his shoulder and hands you one of the cocktails for which he was named Irish National Champion.

MEXICO

San Miguel de Allende

CASA DE SIERRA NEVADA
Hospicio #35
San Miguel de Allende, Guanajuato 37700, Mexico
011-52-415-27040
Bartender: MANUEL "MANNIX" RAMÍREZ

Nestled in the charming town of San Miguel de Allende, in Mexico's colonial central highlands, the Casa de Sierra Nevada is one of the world's finest small luxury hotels, and its bar and restaurant mirror the owners' approach to doing everything right. Mannix, who's been tending bar there for fifteen years, prides himself on his drinks: "I make a dry Martini as good as the best in New York." He's also known for his Margaritas and Sangritas. His Gaby's Cocktail, named after the hotel's vivacious, multilingual concierge, Gabriela Rocha Díaz, is a libationary work of art. If tequila is your thing, they have more than sixty-four varieties from which to choose. And if you ask Mannix (preferably in Spanish), he'll pack you up a thermos of Martinis or Margaritas to enjoy on a picnic at the hotel's five-hundred-acre ranch a few miles outside town.

UNITED STATES

Aspen

THE J BAR, HOTEL JEROME
330 East Main Street
Aspen, CO 81611
970-920-1000
Bartender: GRAYSON STOVER

Silver-rushers "created" Aspen in 1880, and by 1889 Civil War hero Jerome Wheeler had built the Hotel Jerome. The cherrywood J Bar (the colonel had no problems with self-image) dates back to 1889 as well, and it is here you can find all those who succumb to the lure of Aspen, from Lauren Bacall to Calvin Klein, from Bill Clinton to Lee Iaccoca. It has been said that the J Bar *is* Aspen.

Atlanta

FADO IRISH PUB
3035 Peachtree Road
Atlanta, GA 30305
404-841-0066
Bartender: FRANCIS "FRANK" McLOUGHLIN

Opened in January 1996, Fado is the first in a series of Irish pubs being imported to America, the brainchildren of an investment group affiliated with Irish brewing giant Guinness. To walk into Fado is to step inside a pub in the heart of Ireland, authentic in every detail. The group is opening other Irish pubs (some with different names) in Chicago, Austin, Denver, and Stamford, CT.

THE MARTINI CLUB
1140 Crescent Avenue
Atlanta, GA 30030
404-873-0794
Bartenders: CHRISTINA E. MARTIN, KEVIN BENNETT, and
**   "MARTY" MARTINI**

This handsome, upscale Atlanta bar has taken the city by storm since opening in late 1995. "Cigars and Martinis just seem to go together," say the owners, and The Martini Club is an Atlanta haven for lovers of both. There are fifty-four types of Martinis and an extensive upstairs humidor room and cigar bar. Movers and shakers in The South's "Big City" couldn't be happier.

TONGUE & GROOVE
3055 Peachtree Road
Atlanta, GA 30305
404-261-2325
Bartender: MICHAEL HARRIS

Located in the trendy Buckhead area of Atlanta, Tongue & Groove has become one of Atlanta's "in" spots, with celebrities showing up with regularity to enjoy expertly mixed drinks at the club's striking curved bars. The music is jazzy, the patrons are decked out in their tony best, and the merriment lasts into the wee hours.

Beverly Hills

THE CLUB BAR AT THE PENINSULA HOTEL
9882 Santa Monica Boulevard
Beverly Hills, CA 90212
310-551-2888
Bartender: ROBERT SCHWARTZ

The Club Bar mirrors the hotel's elegance and attention to personal detail. Barman Bob Schwartz presides over a stunning room filled with Hollywood's elite, whose favorite bottles are adorned with their names on silver nameplates and whose favorite cigars are properly stored in personalized humidors. The atmosphere is always high tone; the live piano music, well, lively; and the drinks shaken or stirred to perfection.

Boston

BRANDY PETE'S
267 Franklin Street
Boston, MA 02110
617-439-4165
Bartender: JOE MARTIN

Brandy Pete's is a Boston wining-and-dining institution located in the heart of the financial district. Established more than sixty-five years ago by Pete Sabia, who seemed always to have a snifter of brandy in hand when greeting customers, it offers Bostonians handsome decor, straight-ahead food, and drinks made the way they're supposed to be made.

BULL 'N' FINCH PUB ("CHEERS")
The Hampshire House
84 Beacon Street, Boston, MA 02108
617-227-9600
Bartender: EDDIE DOYLE

Arguably the most famous bar in America, thanks to the wildly popular TV show *Cheers,* which used the Bull 'n' Finch as its scenic inspiration. The Bull 'n' Finch is the quintessential warm, comfortable neighborhood bar, presided over for almost twenty-five years by Eddie Doyle. Doyle is considered the "friendliest" bartender in

Boston. When he's not creating the bar's signature drink, the Bloody Mary, he's out raising thousands of dollars for worthy Boston charities.

LOCKE-OBER
3–4 Winter Place
Boston, MA 02108
617-542-1340
Bartender: SATCHA "DANG" HIRANYAKET

A venerable Boston drinking establishment since 1898. The popular drink, the Ward Eight, was invented here in 1901 to celebrate the victory of Martin Lomasney, a popular politician and dedicated teetotaler. Locke-Ober is a hands-down choice for the list of the world's greatest—it was selected by every member of our Boston survey group.

Buffalo

THE ANCHOR BAR
1047 Main Street
Buffalo, NY 14209
716-886-8920
Bartender: IVANO TOSCANI

Mention Buffalo and people are likely to say "the Bills and the Anchor Bar." The Anchor is synonymous with the city, not only because its bar serves up wonderful liquid sources of warmth during the long winters but also because it still whips up what are possibly the world's best Buffalo wings. No surprise—Buffalo wings were invented here.

Chicago

THE PUMP ROOM, OMNI AMBASSADOR EAST HOTEL
1301 N. State Parkway
Chicago, IL 60610
312-266-0360
Bartender: BOB SORENSON

We asked our good friend Jim Villas, esteemed cookbook author and food and wine editor of *Town & Country*, which Chicago bars should be included in this book. Without a nanosecond's hesitation, he said, "The Pump Room!" 'Nuf said.

THE CAPITAL GRILLE
633 North St. Clair Street
Chicago, IL 60611
312-337-9400
Bartender: ROBERT BRADY

Born in Rhode Island and perfected in the nation's capital, Capital Grille steak and chop restaurants invaded Chicago in 1997, and the bar quickly became one of the most popular in town. No wonder. It boasts a Martini menu featuring dozens of vodkas, gins, vermouths, and garnishes, making for a kind of build-your-own-bar for cocktail connoisseurs. The wine list carries more than three hundred selections and awards from *Wine Spectator*.

Dallas

THE MANSION ON TURTLE CREEK
2821 Turtle Creek Boulevard
Dallas, TX 75219
214-559-2100
Bartender: RAY BOND

Does Turtle Creek flow slowly because of its name, or is it named Turtle Creek because it flows slowly? You can sit and ponder that over one of Ray Bond's Mansion Bloody Marys, which—surprise—you'll find you have to chew. It's all veggies, unlike the mammalian heads that adorn the Texas-size walls.

East Hampton, Long Island

THE BLUE PARROT
33A Main Street
East Hampton, NY 11937
516-324-3609
Bartender: ROLAND EISENBERG

Despite being featured in James Brady's recent best-selling novel, *Further Lane*, along with his cigar-smoking dog, Little Bit, which gets mugged, bartender Roland attributes the Blue Parrot's sixteen-year success ("a lifetime in the bar business") to the fact it's been run by "brilliant, good-looking surfers." Long Islander Billy Joel sometimes drops in on a whim to play the piano.

Kansas City

JARDINES JAZZ CLUB
4536 Main Street
Kansas City, MO 64111
816-561-6480
Bartender: BRIAN FINEGOLD

Jardines is Middle America's center for thick steaks and cool jazz, where the profession of bartending is raised to an art, and the Martini is a "blank canvas." It's where those in the know go to sample the latest single malt to hit town and to see who's sipping the most trendy of novelty Martinis: "Dreamcicle, please; make it dry." "Will that be straight up, or on a stick?"

Key West

THE GREEN PARROT
801 Whitehead Street
Key West, FL 33040
305-294-6133
Bartender: VICKI ROUSH with MIKE DELISE

More colorful even than its name, The Green Parrot dubs itself "a sunny place for shady people," where there has been "no sniveling since 1890." It's difficult to imagine what happened to the last patron who sniveled, but he or she probably suffered the same fate as the woman who claimed to be Martha Stewart's personal secretary. The view of Lou Diamond Phillips bending over the pool table, though, was most appreciated by professional bartender Vicki Roush. The first, and last, bar on U.S. Route 1, The Green Parrot is a landmark.

Little Rock

THE CAPITAL HOTEL BAR
111 West Markham Street
Little Rock, AR 72201
501-370-7088
Bartender: KHALIL MOUSSA

President Clinton has enjoyed a drink in this handsome, genteel fixture on the Little Rock social scene. So, too, have dozens of other celebrities, along with the city's regular cadre of movers and shakers. Top professional bartenders are discreet, patient, and have good ears. Barman Khalil Moussa typifies these traits and more.

Los Angeles

THE BAR AT THE HOTEL BEL-AIR
701 Stone Canyon Road
Los Angeles, CA 90077
310-472-1211
Bartender: DON MILLS

Quite simply, our two Los Angeles–area entries on the list of the world's greatest bars—The Bar at the Hotel Bel-Air and The Club Bar at the Peninsula Hotel—set the standard against which all Los Angeles bars must be measured, leaving such former trendsetters as The Polo Lounge in the dust. The Bar at the Hotel Bel-Air is a star-studded Southern California oasis, a place to unwind favored by Hollywood's entertainment elite. Bartender Don Mills has been pleasing patrons at this handsome bar for more than ten years; his signature Bloody Mary, whose recipe he graciously shares with us in this book, is world-class. The bar's plush surroundings make you want to linger forever, or at least until you've run out of movie star elbows to rub. An easy choice for the world's greatest list.

New Orleans

PAT O'BRIEN'S BAR
718 St. Peter Street
New Orleans, LA 70116
504-525-4823
Bartender: TONY NETTLETON

New Orleans restaurant critic Gene Bourg maintains that the Hurricane is "probably the most famous drink in New Orleans." Created at Pat O'Brien's Bar, it and the place itself have enjoyed a decades-long symbiotic relationship that has emboldened Pat's successors to claim that theirs is the "largest volume of business of its size of any other drink establishment in the world." Pat O'Brien's has seven bars in all. We recommend the Main bar.

New York

KENNEDY'S
327 West 57th Street
New York, NY 10019
212-307-1722
Bartender: MAURICE O'CONNELL

Pretty Rose will greet you with a genuine smile and wink and, perhaps, a first round on the house. If you make it to the main dining room, Roy might do the same, but you must first get past the inimitable hospitality of Martin, Herbie, or Paulie, and shake Jonathan's hand before you can sit down to one of the best burgers in New York. Of course, you might not get to sit down anywhere but in the back bar if Maurice sees you coming, and he always does, whether you're from CBS down the street, one of myriad rock stars or politicians who frequent the place, or just a guy from across 57th. Relax, go with the flow, and enjoy New York at its absolute friendliest.

THE BAR AT MORTON'S
551 Fifth Avenue
New York, NY 10017
212-972-3315
Bartender: SEAN McCARTHY

This Chicago eatery, masterminded and deftly guided to national prominence by bon vivant Allen J. Bernstein, moved into The Big Apple a few years ago, and before the new arrivals learned how to pronounce "Noo Yawk," the magazine of the same name gave them kudos for the best steak in town. Here's a tip: Go through the front door off 45th Street and make a hard left. You'll find yourself in the bar, where you should be, with Sean and, if you're lucky, Meaghan. This is where the power brokers of Midtown come to drink straight, smoke strong, talk tough, and then go scream at the Knicks and Rangers.

PETE'S TAVERN
129 East 18th Street
New York, NY 10003
212-473-7676
Bartender: GARY EGAN

If Pete's Tavern isn't the oldest bar in Manhattan, it comes close. It's the quintessential free-standing neighborhood saloon in a big neighborhood; people flock there from the five boroughs and beyond. Its bartender, Gary Egan, has been serving up locals and tourists for more than ten years, and he's as sure in his movements behind the scarred bar as he is in making the perfect drink every time. Pete's Tavern represents New York City as it used to be, which is nice.

THE RAINBOW ROOM
30 Rockefeller Plaza
New York, NY 10112
212-632-5000
Bartender: DALE DeGROFF

Enjoying an expertly made drink sixty-five floors up over Manhattan is like sipping cocktails aboard an ocean liner headed for Europe. The entire "Rainbow" complex, occupying two floors atop Rockefeller Plaza, is, well, spectacular. You've seen Dale DeGroff, its beverage director, on dozens of TV shows. Considered by many to be New York's foremost mixologist, he is a purist and a collector of vintage cocktail and prohibition literature. One of the world's greatest bars? Without a doubt. Not surprising with Joe Baum's creative, innovative hand at the helm.

THE "21" CLUB
21 West 52nd Street
New York, NY 10019
212-582-7200
Bartender: MICHAEL SHANNON

America's most famous surviving speakeasy. Its legend never stops growing as it continues to serve the rich and famous in its own unique style. The tone is distinctly elegant, yet relaxed. Customers feel like members of a club, even if they've never been there before. (It's the only bar at which a guy from Kentucky ever tried to sell us a racehorse.) Never had a drink at "21"? Shame on you. Mike Shannon, as professional a barman as has ever been born to the task, has been serving presidents, film icons, and Manhattan high rollers for years. Order a drink and watch closely; it's like going to bartender college.

WINDOWS ON THE WORLD
One World Trade Center, 107th Floor
New York, NY 10048
212-524-7000
Bartender: MARIE MAHER

When a bartender has her own custom business cards, you know she's among the elite of mixologists. Marie Maher has earned that status; customers keep coming back to the bar because they know they'll receive the perfect drink, served with class. The bar itself is billed as "The Greatest Bar on Earth." An overstatement? A reach? Probably not, although we're certain a few others on our list of the world's greatest might challenge it. But there's no debate that enjoying a drink here has to rank up there with other great life experiences.

WOLLENSKY'S GRILL
205 East 49th Street
New York, NY 10017
212-753-0444
Bartender: PATRICK FORD

There are a couple of writers who have hung out at the end of the bar here for so long that somebody has painted them and hung the image on the wall. Of course, the painting makes less noise, which is what makes it easy to distinguish one from the other. Patrick, on the other hand, is a gentleman and a scholar who nightly can inspire even writers to contribute to a scholarship for a needy patron. Wollensky's customers tend to be big, bright men and beautiful, brilliant women in search of nothing but a good time at the bar. Who could ask for more?

Philadelphia

DICKENS INN
421 S. Second Street
Philadelphia, PA 19147
215-928-0232
Bartender: JERRY SUROWICZ

Charles Dickens was a master of setting a scene and then shifting the point of view, and shifting it again, as if he were anticipating the advent of the motion picture. It is impossible to read Dickens and not get yanked into the story, dragged across the dimly lit cobblestone streets, and . . . end up at the Dickens Inn. Bartender Jerry Surowicz had his point of view shifted when a fellow walked in and introduced himself as Cedric Charles Dickens, great grandson of the author. Surely he must have felt at home, with the dark woods, English drafts, and images of Dickens characters with each shift of view. Talk about name-dropping.

Portland

HIGGINS RESTAURANT AND BAR
1239 SW Broadway
Portland, OR 97205
503-222-9070
Bartender: PAUL MALLORY

With chef Jonathan Kiewel creating masterpieces in the kitchen, bartender Paul Mallory has his hands full keeping up the bar end of Higgins Restaurant and Bar. He manages handsomely. It was a fellow from Holland, Michigan (of all places), who first recommended Higgins to us with wild-eyed enthusiasm. If your sweet tooth is throbbing, be sure to order a Chocolate Martini, and don't even ask what Michael Jordan drinks when he's trailblazing Portland.

San Francisco

THE BUENA VISTA
2765 Hyde Street
San Francisco, CA 94109
415-474-5044
Bartender: BILL SNOW

Irish coffee was first introduced to Americans in this hopping bistro, located at the turntable for the Hyde Street cable car line on Fisherman's Wharf. The tables are communal; there's no greater spot in the world for meeting like-minded people. The bartenders crank out thousands of Irish coffees a day, along with other house specialty drinks like chilled Aalborg akvavit with a "snit" of beer, New Orleans Fizz, and Tequila Sangrita. The Buena Vista is one of the authors' personal favorites on the list of the world's greatest.

THE COMPASS ROSE BAR,
THE WESTIN ST. FRANCIS HOTEL

335 Powell Street
San Francisco, CA 94102
415-774-0167
Bartender: DANNY WOO

Is The Compass Rose Bar the most elegant, sedate bar in America? You'll receive no argument from us. It's truly an "event" bar, pouring more champagne than any other establishment in California. Barman Danny Woo has been there for more than fourteen years and mirrors the management's quiet approach to providing well-dressed patrons the perfect drink in perfect surroundings.

THE TOP OF THE MARK, THE MARK HOPKINS HOTEL
Number One Nob Hill
San Francisco, CA 94108
415-392-3434
Bartender: HANK WILLIAM CANCEL

Millions of visitors have sat at the expanse of windows in this American treasure and watched the famed San Francisco fog engulf the Golden Gate Bridge while sipping their favorite cocktail. Bartender Hank William Cancel has a bag of bartending tricks he was willing to share with us, and we've shared them with you. The Top of the Mark is a great bar in a great city. Put having a drink there on your "before I die" list.

Seattle

QUEEN CITY GRILL
2201 First Avenue
Seattle, WA 98121
206-443-0975
Bartender: KEVIN STEWART

We asked our survey group in this lovely city to recommend bars to be included on our list. It was unanimous: The Queen City Grill had to be included. It serves up superb drinks and pleases customers in its downtown location. Kevin Stewart, who has been behind the bar there for seven years, is a walking primer on Seattle's myriad microbrewery ales and beers.

RAY'S BOATHOUSE
6049 Seaview Avenue, NW
Seattle, WA 98107
206-789-3770
Bartender: PATRICK NEGRON

The ice-cold Blueberry Daiquiris numb the throat as you sit on the expansive deck, breathe in the pristine Seattle air, and watch the ships pass through the locks below. Inside, the bar hops day and night, and for good reason: The bartenders, led by Patrick Negron, are masters of the bartending profession and take pride (as all the bartenders who've contributed to this book do) in their knowledge and skill. A Seattle mainstay, and deserving of that designation.

St. Louis

HARRY'S RESTAURANT AND BAR
2144 Market Street
St. Louis, MO 63103
314-421-6969
Bartender: RICHARD ROSS

The patio can seat 350 people, and the staff never bat an eye when the crush is on. Richard Ross and his bartending colleagues expertly juggle thirty-eight single-malt Scotches, nineteen varieties of Port, and thirty wines from California, along with all the mixed drinks they're called upon to blend. A first-class bar, with the St. Louis skyline as its backdrop.

Washington, DC

THE LIBRARY LOUNGE, THE CARLTON HOTEL
923 16th & K Streets, NW
Washington, DC 20006
202-638-2626, Ext. 6719
Bartender: NATHAN YU

Not as well known as many other venerable Washington watering holes, but one of that city's finest examples of how an upscale bar should be run. The atmosphere is as elegant as the bar service, and Nathan Yu's secrets for providing quality drinks are shared with us in this book. There are lots of them, but they all start with one rule: "Buy and use only the best." Can't argue with that.

The Sky

VIRGIN ATLANTIC AIRWAYS
800-862-8621

We couldn't resist including an airline on our list of the world's fifty greatest bars because Virgin Atlantic's approach to serving cocktails in the lounge of its fleet of 747s is unmatched in the airline industry. But that's to be expected, considering this airline's commitment to excellence in everything it does, including Virgin vodka (which calls to mind a conundrum: How long can a vodka remain virginal, if only in name?).

MAY THE SPIRITS
BE WITH YOU

GIN

Gin, a spirit synonymous with the classic Martini, has what might be called a sordid past.

Dutch Gin

It was first introduced in the seventeenth century by Dutch chemist Franciscus de la Boe, who mixed alcohol with juniper to create *jenever*, a tonic for those suffering kidney problems. Whether it had any medicinal effect on the kidneys is conjecture, but it undoubtedly made patients feel better, if only because they forgot what ailed them.

The juniper blend blossomed when William III, the Dutch monarch, married England's Mary II and became King of England in 1689. He wasn't especially fond of the French, who had designs on Holland, and he slapped high excise taxes on French brandies and wines. Bingo! Dutch jenever was imported in large quantities to England, an economic boost to Holland and a source of inexpensive alcohol for Englishmen.

The problem was that by the eighteenth century, Britain's burgeoning lower class liked the new concoction too much to suit certain civic-minded members of the upper class. Prime Minister Gladstone did his best to prohibit the sale of gin, and the Salvation Army was created, in part, to wean the population off this destructive threat to English civilization.

The poor drowned their sorrows in pubs, where they often mixed gin with milk, giving it the unflattering nickname "mother's milk." It was called even worse things. Because juniper berries spawned a classic old wives' tale that they induced abortions, gin also became known as "mother's ruin." English citizens living what was considered an unsavory life were said to be living on "Gin Lane." And members of the military, drinking it on the eve of battle, labeled it "Dutch courage."

Quite a history for an alcoholic spirit that has since come to symbolize sophistication, wealth, and ultimate good taste when contained in an elegant martini glass.

British Gin

Originally, gin was a sweet concoction, generally known as Old Tom Gin. But British distillers went to work to improve and refine the flavor, adding to the juniper berries such herbs as lemon or bitter Bigarade orange peels, felle, cassias bark, caraway, coriander, orris, angelica, licorice, Indian cardamom seed, and anise. At the same time, they perfected a slow distilling process utilizing continuous stills, and what's called "rectification," the ability to purify the malted barley that forms the basis for all gin. The result was the dry gin we know and love today.

The differences in the taste of various dry gins has to do with each distiller's blending of herbs and juniper; they guard their recipes with all the zeal of a cornered honey badger.

Eventually, British gin lovers began coating their glasses with either French or Italian vermouth before adding the gin. They called it Gin-and-French or Gin-and-It. We know it as the Classic Martini.

Actually, gin truly made its mark on the world in British-ruled India, where quinine, a bitter substance given daily to the troops to ward off malaria, tasted better when gin was added. This practice gave birth to Gin and Tonic, which continues to this day to be a popular drink in the heat of summer, whether malaria threatens or not. Tonic, of course, achieves its unique taste because of the quinine in it.

The British also invented pink gin, which became quite popular with a segment of the aristocracy. Actually, it's nothing more than dry gin allowed to stand in a shaker with angostura bitters, which turns the gin a pinkish color.

Choosing Gin for the Home Bar

The home bartender has many excellent choices. Most leading brands—Boodles, Bombay, Tanqueray, Beefeater, and others—are British. But there are Dutch and Irish gins available, too. Bols Genever is a Dutch brand found in larger liquor stores in America. And an Irish gin lauded by many, Cork Dry Gin, is also available in the United States.

An important word about buying gin for your home bar: Our panel of professional bartenders all agree that a properly stocked bar should consist primarily of premium, "top-shelf" brands. This is especially true of gin and vodka that will be used to make Martinis. Unlike many mixed drinks, in which other ingredients can serve to mask lesser-quality liquor, gin and vodka stand alone in Martinis, with only a hint of vermouth. The flavor of the gin or vodka dominates: gin or vodka of inferior quality will quickly be discerned, but not appreciated, by your Martini-loving guests.

The authors know a few people of questionable character who put inferior brands of liquor into empty premium brand bottles in order to impress guests. They should be condemned to a perpetual hangover. We also know another fellow who buys the cheapest gin and adds a few drops of Scotch to it, claiming it "smoothes it out" to the extent that his guests won't taste the bathtub variety's harshness. In addition to his hangover, we wish him terminal prickly heat.

Gin is important to one of the authors, whose mother put a little of it in his bottle each night to help him sleep. (He was a good baby.) To this day, the taste of gin ranks as one of his most pleasurable experiences, so much so that before he has his first of the day, always with a few teaspoons of freshly squeezed lemon juice, he first brushes his teeth to provide a clean palate for the gin to play upon.

VODKA

One of the reasons for vodka's popularity remains unknown to many who enjoy it the most: As vodka travels through one's digestive system, it delivers relatively few hangover-causing ingredients. Another reason vodka doesn't hurt as much as whiskey is that it is often consumed with food.

While Russian tradition dictates that vodka should accompany food, most Americans satisfy that convention by throwing down a handful of pretzels or peanuts with their V&Ts or Sea Breezes. But we should all enjoy, at least once in our lifetime, using a mother-of-pearl spoon to spread a mound of beluga caviar over a perfect toast point (if you must, add a touch of chopped egg, another of chopped onion, and a hint of sour cream), savoring it for as long as we can stand, and then sipping a frozen Stoli before ever degrading vodka as a drink to be swilled.

We should catch an ornery salmon on a fly, say a blessing over it, fillet it, grill it with a brush of olive oil and a squeeze of lemon, fork off a good-size chunk, and chow it down, followed by a mouthful of Absolut Citron, before arguing about which wine goes best with a fish we've fought. With new vodkas like Skyy and Ketel One popping up like potato puffs and vodka bars proliferating like McDonald's restaurants, the trend has degenerated into a fad, and it's too bad. Vodka is the most cocktailizable of all the liquors (and as such, it should command as much respect as a fine olive oil). It is the basic ingredient of more drinks in this book than any other. Good vodka can make a fine dry Martini. Bad vodka can help make a killer Long Island Iced Tea. Need we say more?

Vodka is generally acknowledged to have been created by Russian peasants, who distilled it from potatoes. The Poles and the Ukrainians (never argue with a Ukrainian) claim the birthright as well, and the Ukrainians produce a convincing Perlova as an exclamation point.

Now, wheat and other grains are used in its production, and an increasing volume is distilled in the United States—currently the world's leading producer.

As with all spirits, the quality of the water contributes significantly to the quality of the final product, and vodkas can vary. Appropriately enough, the word *vodka* comes from the Russian word for "water," *voda*. The "ka" defines it more succinctly as "little water." To be entirely correct, the translation is "darling little water."

Some of the most sensual drinks ever concocted have been created around vodka, including the Blue Lagoon, the Fuzzy Navel, Lovers' Nocturne, the Slow Comfortable Screw, and, of course, the Stupid Cupid. (We won't even whisper the words "Screaming Orgasm.")

Since its inception in Russia (we can't find proof to the contrary) in the 1300s, vodka has probably made millions of would-be Cupids stupid, and today its bootlegging in that country has cost the government millions of dollars a day in lost tax revenues. Russians who have come to consider their little water a staple of life seem to become increasingly defiant with each *"Na zdorovia"* or "to your health" they proffer.

For whatever reason, the United States legislates that vodkas produced here must be colorless, odorless, and tasteless. While they are not completely, it is this near neutrality that makes them so versatile. They assume, some say enhance, the taste of whatever fruit they are mixed with.

Worldwide, however, vodka has become its own symbol of bottled irony. It is a spirit that, ideally, is distilled to a point of flavorlessness. Yet it proliferates in an absurd variety of flavor-added mixtures, from Absolut Peppar to Stoli Vanil. But we can't come down too hard on vodka additives because some are very good (Absolut Citron and Stoli Ohranj come to palate) and because it was the Russians who started the trend. Even Peter peppered his vodka on his road to Greatness. Russians have been adding seeds, grass, and herbs to their vodkas since long before we were able to drink or reason. (Is that an oxymoron?)

Because it is distilled like whiskey, vodka was known in the United States during World War II as white whiskey, and it did, in fact, follow its flavorful white cousin, gin, as the potent ingredient in the

Bloody Mary. More about that later. Vodka is distilled at 100 proof—higher than most whiskeys—and neutral spirits are charcoal filtered—sometimes as many as three times. Then, traditionally, distilled water is added to reduce the vodka to 80 proof.

Vodkas differ according to the starting ingredient, most commonly corn, then wheat; in Turkey, even beets are used, which could be great fodder for a punster. It's been a while since the first Russian peasants dreamed up the idea of making booze from potatoes, but things that go around come around, and there is one American distillery today making vodka from potatoes. One guess as to its name—the Idaho Vodka Distillery!

Odd, isn't it, how fiercely brand-loyal vodka drinkers can be to products that are defined by the Bureau of Alcohol, Tobacco, and Firearms to be " . . . without distinctive character, aroma, taste, or color." In 1994, the *Washingtonian* magazine conducted a blind vodka tasting. American-made, inexpensive Popov won. The following year, one of the most expensive vodkas on the shelf, Stolichnaya Cristall, was judged best. James Bond was on neither panel of judges, preferring to sip his fetchingly neat (thanks to Ian Fleming) vodka Martini on a yacht. The findings, by the way, are available in the January 1996 *Washingtonian* and at Washingtonian On-Line.

WHISKEY/WHISKY

The term *whiskey*, with and without the "e," denotes a wide variety of alcoholic beverages, the common denominator of which is grain: All whiskeys, including bourbon and Scotch, are produced from distilling various grains. It's the specific grain used, the distilling process, the way certain types are blended, and, as with bourbon, the water that distinguishes one whiskey from another.

We can thank our Gaelic ancestors for whiskey. The word itself comes from the Gaelic term *usquebaugh* or *eau de vie*, "water of life." But although whiskey is not an American invention, we've added enough twists to it to be able to claim part ownership.

The production of all whiskeys involves basically the same process. First the grain is ground and then cooked with water to release the starch. The cooked grain is rinsed and the liquid containing the starch, called *wort*, is strained off. The spent grain, or "mash," is usually used for animal feed. Cultured yeast is introduced to the wort, initiating fermentation. Out of that emerges an alcoholic liquid known as beer. Then comes the distilling stage of whiskey making. The beer is distilled either in what's called a pot still or in a continuous still, producing what we know as whiskey.

All whiskey has to be watered down to lower the proof. The proof of any distilled spirit indicates the percentage of alcohol by volume. An 80-proof whiskey has 40 percent alcohol by volume. Ninety-proof whiskey has 45 percent alcohol. Simple to remember: The alcohol potency of any whiskey is half what the proof says on the label. Divide the proof in half and you know how much alcohol is in the bottle.

The aging of whiskey takes place in a variety of barrel types. For bourbon, it's new, charred oak casks. Other whiskeys age in used barrels purchased from bourbon distillers.

That's pretty much it. Various distillers will add a spin on the process, claiming their method results in superior whiskey. Maybe it does. What's important is that when stocking your home bar with spirits, be discerning about what you buy. You may find great buys on certain whiskeys that will do nicely in mixed drinks. But as our participating bartenders from the world's greatest bars *all* preach, go for top-shelf, and proudly display those impressive bottles behind your home bar. The difference in cost between inferior whiskey (inferior spirits of all types, for that matter) and premium brands isn't that much in the overall scheme of things, and you simply can't go wrong serving your guests the best.

What kinds of whiskey are we apt to include in our well-stocked bar? Let's begin with American-made whiskey.

The British might have done us a huge favor during the Revolutionary War when they blockaded the delivery of Caribbean rum to the American colonies. That inspired some enterprising American entrepreneurs to begin making whiskey, utilizing all the barley and rye we had on hand. As the colonies expanded westward, corn became a popular grain for use in whiskey making, spawning the development of "America's whiskey"—bourbon.

Types of Whiskey

Today, when the home bartender walks into his or her favorite local liquor store, there are myriad choices in whiskeys. But they come down to basically six types:

- Bourbon
- Scotch
- Rye
- Irish Whiskey
- Canadian Whisky
- Blends

There are, of course, variations on the theme. Tennessee whiskey must, by law, come from Tennessee. And corn whiskey has to have been distilled with no less than 80 percent corn. Corn whiskey is not in the same class as bourbon, although it has its fervent admirers.

Bourbon

Bourbon is distinctly American, so much so that in 1965, Congress passed a resolution classifying it as a distinctive national product. Unsophisticated home bartenders sometimes consider bourbon just another whiskey, interchangeable with rye or Canadian. Not so. Bourbon has a distinctive taste, and to substitute another whiskey when the recipe calls for bourbon is a little like saying any old spice will do when preparing a meal.

Our professional bartenders follow a set of inviolate rules, which we present throughout the book. One of them is that when a recipe calls for a particular liquor, that's the liquor that must be used. Which is not to say that you can't experiment. But do it when you're the one sampling your own creative effort. For guests, follow recipes to the letter, and that includes using the alcoholic beverage called for.

Bourbon is not only American, it's synonymous with the state of Kentucky. You can buy bourbons distilled elsewhere, but the best have always come from the Bluegrass State. Kentucky bourbon has a rich, identifiable flavor resulting from its main ingredient, corn; from Kentucky's water, which filters through extensive limestone formations; and from the charred new oak casks in which bourbon is aged.

By law, Bourbon must contain no less than 51 percent corn. And unlike other casks in which whiskey is aged, the charred barrels used for bourbon must never be utilized a second time—at least not for bourbon distillation. Most of them are sold after their one-time use to distillers of single-malt Scotch.

Single-Barrel Bourbon

While single-malt Scotch has gained considerable popularity in America, single-barrel bourbon has been slower to catch on. But it's getting there, and for the same good reason single-malt Scotch has captured the palates of discerning drinkers: It tastes better. It's that simple. Don't misunderstand. Top-shelf blended bourbons are superb whiskeys, worthy of being enjoyed au naturel in a balloon snifter. But single-barrel bourbon has a character all its own.

Making bourbon, including the single-barrel variety, involves five basic stages. It's the final step in the process that distinguishes single-barrel from blended bourbon.

First, the grains are ground into a meal, which is heated with water to convert the solid mass of starch into a soluble substance. Most of the grain used for bourbon is corn, of course; the other grains are added for seasoning.

Second, a "mashing machine" homogenizes the thick, gooey liquid known as beer, which is recycled several times.

Third, the fermentation process is begun by adding yeast to help convert the sugars to alcohol, which takes between three and four days.

Fourth is distillation, during which the alcohol, which is extracted from the beer, is continuously boiled as it passes through the perforated plates of a large steel column—the still. When the beer reaches the bottom of the column, the alcohol has burned off, leaving behind water and solids. The liquid is now transferred to large tanks and then pumped into new charred oak barrels.

Fifth is the maturation or aging stage, when the bourbon "mellows out." Here's where single-barrel bourbon parts company with other bourbons destined to be blended. Blending allows some room for error in taste. Not so with single-barrel. Master distillers must decide, based upon their experience (there's no gauge announcing when aging is completed), precisely when to proclaim any given barrel to be ready for bottling.

Sour Mash Whiskey

Before indulging in a little bourbon history, a word about sour mash whiskey, confused by some people with bourbon. Actually, sour mash *is* a form of bourbon. But don't try to pawn it off on a guest expecting bourbon. The taste is very different. What happens when sour mash is made is that some mash that's already been used in previous distillation, "sour mash," is added to the fresh mash about to be processed.

Southern Comfort

We also might as well comment on Southern Comfort in this section because it does involve bourbon. Years ago, someone began marinating fresh peaches in bourbon and called the drink—why, we don't know— Cuffs and Buttons. Genteel Southern women liked it because it mitigated the strong taste of straight bourbon. It became so popular that a distiller started marketing it under the trademarked name Southern Comfort.

While a few mixed-drink recipes call for Southern Comfort, it's more commonly served as a cordial because of its inherent sweetness.

Bourbon History

Why is bourbon distilled only in charred oak barrels? We've heard a few explanations, but the one we prefer to believe concerns a frugal Scottish immigrant and early bourbon distiller. A number of white oak staves used to make barrels were accidentally charred in a fire. The thought of discarding them was anathema; instead, our Scotsman went ahead and made the barrels but put the burned sides of the staves inside to hide their blemishes. When he emptied those barrels after his bourbon had aged in them, he realized the charred wood had taken the bite out of the whiskey and had given it a pleasant russet color. From that moment on, he burned his staves.

Some say casks were deliberately burned because they'd originally contained fish or molasses. No matter what the genesis of charred oak casks, if whiskey isn't aged in charred barrels, it can't be called bourbon.

One bourbon "fact" seems to be accepted by just about every historian: The first bourbon to come out of a charred cask was distilled by the Reverend Elijah Craig of Georgetown, Kentucky, in 1789.

Other Bourbon Trivia

President Abraham Lincoln worked as a lad in a bourbon distillery operated by his dad.

The ritual of ending each legislative day with bourbon and branch water was popular in Congress during the administration of Franklin Delano Roosevelt, 32nd president of the United States. Vice President John Nance Garner often encouraged the Senate to adjourn early to, as he put it, "strike a blow for liberty."

Perhaps bourbon contributed to FDR's sense of humor when he ordered one hundred copies of a certain edition of the *Washington Post* after the paper ran a headline that read, instead of "President in Bed with a Cold," "President in Bed with a Coed."

Mark Twain's love of Kentucky bourbon was well known. He never traveled without his trusty bottle, causing an occasional run-in with customs inspectors. Once, when an inspector found a bottle of bourbon in Twain's suitcase that the humorist claimed contained only clothing, he responded, "It's the truth, sir. That is my much needed nitecap."

During one trip to London, Mark Twain's visit to the Savage Club outlasted his supply of bourbon. Hearing of this calamity, British friends obtained two cases from an importer and presented them to the author "as a testimonial of admiration and affection." A few days later, a telegram forced Twain to cut short his stay and to leave behind his two cases of bourbon. "I will be back very shortly," he told the Savage Club management. "Save them for me. Let no one touch them while I am gone."

Twain never returned to the Savage Club, but the proprietors respected his wish. Shortly before the club was destroyed during World

War II, a reporter from the *Detroit Free Press*, Malcolm Bingay, heard the story and decided to see for himself it if was true. The club's manager led him to a subbasement where Bingay found the two cases wrapped in heavy oilcloth. A large label read: "Property of Samuel L. Clemens (Mark Twain)." Bingay informed the manager that Twain was dead.

"That matters not, sir. He told us to keep them here until he returned. And that we shall do."

Only Luftwaffe bombs were able to break that promise.

It's no wonder that bourbon marinated much of Twain's humor. It has always been an intrinsic element of Americana. "Westward the star of empire takes its way," was a popular nineteenth-century saying along the American frontier. Twain changed it to, "Westward the jug of empire takes its way."

More bourbon was consumed during Prohibition than in any other period in history, contributing much to the legend of speakeasies, flappers, and Elliot Ness. Many a bourbon-based cocktail was conceived and named during that era.

SCOTCH: PAMPERED PURITY

Scottish folk had been smacking their lips over their namesake whisky (without the "e") for about a thousand years before they started sharing it with the rest of us in the mid-nineteenth century. The distillation of Scotch whisky was very much a cottage industry until the Glenlivet Distillery was granted a license in 1824. Since then, Scotch whisky has become a critically important industry, a prime export, and a symbol of Scotland as recognizable as the kilt.

Making Scotch Whisky

Scotch whisky begins with the making of barley malt. The barley grain is soaked in water for two or three days, spread two to three feet deep on a stone floor until it begins to germinate, and then turned over repeatedly each time roots begin to show.

The germinated barley is then dried in a kiln over a smoking peat fire to the desired degree of smokiness and then allowed to finish drying over coal heat. The malted barley is left to rest for several weeks, then the rootlets are removed and the grain ground. The ground barley is mixed with hot water to produce wort, which is cooled and poured into an oak vat. Yeast is then added to the wort and the maltose first converted to dextrose, then to alcohol and water. This mixture of yeast, water, and alcohol is called the "wash."

The wash is distilled in an enclosed tank with a long spout. The alcohol boils before the water does, vaporizes up the spout, and drips into a vat.

Scotch History

Distilling wonderful malt Scotch whisky takes cool clear water as well as time and patience. While the peat and water have surely abounded in Scotland for millennia, most able-bodied Scots—from the time their activities were recorded until 1603, when James VI of Scotland also became James I of England—occupied much of their time warding off Viking invasions from the north and English assaults from the south. A self-respecting Scotsman would barely have time to turn over his first forkful of germinating barley before he'd be having to stick the pitchfork into the point-man of one marauding horde or another. Hence, the gentle art of distilling, like those of brewing and winemaking, was carried on by friars in abbeys.

With the Reformation in the sixteenth century, these out-of-work monks had to find some way to make a living, and many put their spirit-making skills to work. The product of tranquil abbeys, having found its way north to the Highlands, was soon being blamed as the fuel that flamed many a barbaric clan feud.

Before long, the inevitable subject of taxation arose, giving rise, itself, to the inevitable criminal pursuits of evasion and smuggling, which proved to be far more efficient and effective than any governmental effort at enforcement. Scotch would remain for centuries a source of acrimony and rows between the English and the Scots. In 1725, taxes on malt and ale led to riots in Glasgow and well-founded charges that the taxes from the south on the products of the north violated the union agreement between England and Scotland that had been timorously struck eighteen years before.

It wasn't until the nineteenth century that taxation and licensing controls began to transform Scotch from a cottage-industry product into an internationally traded and widely sought commodity of distinction. Most impressive is the popularity it achieved in the United States in the middle of this century, when it became the alcoholic beverage of choice among Americans. Having since been superseded by vodka, Scotch has rebounded recently with the growing popularity of tasty, and pricey, single malts.

Single-Malt Scotch

A single malt comes from only one distillery, or even from only one barrel, in which case it is then a "single-single." In fact, there is a Scotch Malt Whisky Society that costs $149 to join. Its purpose is " . . . to promote the appreciation and discerning consumption of the finest whisky in the world."

More than one hundred distilleries throughout Scotland produce malts distinctive unto themselves, including Bowmore, which makes a forty-year-old single malt. Last year only 294 bottles were made, with 60 of them shipped to the United States. They went for $7,000 a bottle. Bowmore also offers a thirty-year-old version, which will set you back only about $200.

It is truly remarkable how different single-malt Scotches can taste. One of the primary reasons for these distinctions is the varying shapes of the pot stills. No two are the same. And depending upon what it flows through, and over, water helps determine the taste of Scotch whisky. If it flows through peat, it will add to the smokiness of the drink; granite-based streams will proffer a smoother taste.

The hard core of Scotch whisky is Speyside, which suggests the importance of water in the blend. Here the River Spey and its tributaries are tapped to be drunk much later by many an appreciative palate around the world.

In the Highlands, the primary area of Scotch production, even the broiling, blustery, blowing salt sea blends its own flavors into the stony character of the malts, not to mention what it adds to those produced on the isle of Islay. Which brings us to why Scotch is, and should be, a decreasingly used ingredient in cocktails. Single-malt Scotch, like single-barrel bourbon, should not be mixed with anything—even ice. It should be deftly poured into a fine, buffed-clean glass, swirled to extract its aroma, sniffed, sipped, savored momentarily on the palate, and swallowed like the gift it is. If you care to show it the respect it is truly due, you'll turn the glass upside down, light a lighter beneath the rim, and cook out any unwanted odors before treating the container to three ounces (we joyfully part here with British bureaucracy) of pampered purity.

In the United States, one of the most reliable sources of single-malt Scotches is the tiny Park Avenue Liquor Shop, located oddly enough at 292 Madison Avenue in New York City.

Those who enjoy good single malts, and who also like to travel, might want to swagger the Whisky Trail through the heartland of Scotland's malt-producing Speyside region. This Highland fling along the foothills of the Grampians could take a weekend or a week and should be attempted only with the services of a designated driver. Taste them all—but bring home a Macallan.

Rye

Like bourbon, which must be made with at least 51 percent corn, rye whiskey must contain no less than 51 percent rye. We suggest you not seek out a straight rye whiskey, one that contains no other grains. A few distilleries make it, but it has a piquant taste that doesn't please most palates. Look for respected brands of blended rye whiskey into which corn, barley, or other grains have been introduced.

Irish Whiskey

Irish whiskey is made pretty much the way Scotch is, with one important exception: The distinctive smoky taste of Scotch is a result of drying its main ingredient, barley malt, over peat fires. The Irish take a different approach: The green barley is not dried over peat (some isn't malted at all), resulting in a vastly different taste. Irish whiskey is one of those spirits you either love or can do without. Suggestion: Have a bottle of top-shelf Irish whiskey always on hand. You may not use it for a long time, but when you're entertaining a prospective client named Mulligan or O'Shea or Brady, and he asks, "You wouldn't have any Irish whiskey, would you?" proudly display the bottle that's been there for what seems forever, smile, and say, "Neat, I assume." You will score major points.

Canadian Whisky

Because Canadian distillers have access to and use greater quantities of wheat in their whiskies, the resulting taste tends to be lighter and more subtle in flavor than Scotch or bourbon. Canadian law doesn't dictate what percentage of any given grain must be used, and American import laws say that all Canadian whisky has to be labeled "blended," as opposed to straight. There is a legion of drinkers who drink nothing but Canadian whisky because of its lighter flavor and, in many cases, lower alcohol content. Don't disappoint them when they visit your home bar.

Blends

Blended whiskies, which account for almost half of all whiskey available on the American market, consist of a minimum of 20 percent straight whiskey that is blended with neutral grain spirits, which have neither flavor, color, nor useful aroma. In this age of single-barrel bourbon and single-malt Scotch whiskies, the uninformed look down on blends. Don't be one of them. A good blended whiskey is perfectly acceptable in a wide variety of mixed drinks.

RUM

We've been to Dead Man's Chest in the Virgin Islands and, like a million other Robert Louis Stevenson fans before us, we've hoisted a bottle of Cruzan and roared, "Fifteen men on a dead man's chest . . . Yo ho ho and a bottle of rum," then sailed on to Norman Island trying to impress each other that we knew, for a fact, that it is the island upon which the master based *Treasure Island*.

Drink enough rum and your sentences do tend to run on. But rum is the laid-back drink, the slick-sippin' liquor that has drawn out the verses of singer/songwriter Jimmy Buffet himself.

Rum History

Rum, like a rebel *with* a cause, rose up in the seventeenth century from the rough-hewn dockside belt-em-back reputation of Barbados, where it was dubbed "Kill Divill," eventually assuming the name (coined locally, recognized worldwide) Mount Gay Sugar Cane Brandy. Once it was called "hellish"; now it's called "very special old reserved." Rum truly is in the eye of the beholder. Then again, rum truly is not what it used to be.

While most objective historians credit Barbados for having distilled the first rum in the mid-seventeenth century, Puerto Rico, 500 miles to the north, claims to have been a half century ahead of the Crown colony. That dispute will never be settled, but we can toss some crushed ice on the sort of row that occasionally flares up when the rums of Puerto Rico claim to "set the standard by which all other rums are judged, worldwide." Our advice? Set your own standard.

The derivation of the word *rum* is in question. One of our erudite bartenders points to the Latin word *saccharum*, meaning "sugar." Not a bad guess. While gin and whiskey owe their existence to grain, rum is the offspring of sugar, pure and simple.

It is more likely that the word *rum* derives from the British Royal Navy's practice back in the late seventeenth century and early eighteenth century of giving its sailors a daily half-pint of rum to combat scurvy. It was questionable medical protocol, considering that scurvy is caused by a lack of vitamin C. But the sailors enjoyed the smooth taste and pleasant aftershocks of their prescribed pleasure, and might well have applied the British slang term *rum* to the brew: "He's a rum lad," meaning he's a pretty good guy but a little on the wild side.

Rum has played a role in American history, not always with laudatory results. New England merchants developed a lucrative business in transporting black American slaves to the Caribbean to work the sugar fields there. In return, they were given molasses, which they brought back to New England for the purpose of making rum. (Yes, for many years there was a thriving rum-distilling business in New England based upon this barbaric practice.) The rum was then traded to American slave owners for more slaves, who were taken to the Caribbean in exchange for more molasses. Called the "Triangle Trade," it represents a dark period in our history.

The famous Boston Tea Party of 1773 wasn't all about tea. Besides tea, the British government also imposed taxes on molasses, the basic ingredient in rum, and rumrunners from the Caribbean broke the British naval blockade during the Revolutionary War.

The political spin doctors for George Washington dispensed generous amounts of rum to voters during the father of our country's bid for the presidency.

There are three basic types of rum. Well, actually there are four if you include what's called "aromatic rum." We prefer to leave it at three. Or even two.

Making Rum

Rum of all varieties follows a basic process. Stalks of raw sugarcane are squeezed between rollers until all the juice has been extracted. This juice is boiled to remove impurities and to clarify it. The resulting thick liquid is put into large stainless-steel machines that whip it around until the sugar itself is separated from the residue, which is black-strap molasses. (Early Spanish settlers stumbled by chance upon what happens to molasses when it's left in the burning Caribbean sun: It naturally ferments. All they had to do was distill it into glorious rum.)

The resulting molasses is boiled to remove impurities and diluted with water. It is combined with water and yeast, fermented, and then distilled. The fermentation period depends on the type of rum.

Light Rum

Light, or clear, rum is the high-tech product of stainless-steel distilling and offers up a subtle, more sophisticated—or less hearty, depending on your taste—flavor.

Puerto Rican rum is the best-known light rum, although buying a bottle with a label proclaiming it's from Puerto Rico doesn't ensure it will be light, any more than a Jamaican rum will necessarily be dark and strongly flavored. Actually, Cuba probably developed the original light rum; it's the home of the famous Bacardi brand.

Bacardi, by the way, is not literally a rum. Rum, in its classic sense, must be made from molasses. Light Cuban or Puerto Rican rums are distilled directly from the fermented sap from the sugarcane itself before it becomes molasses. A minor distinction, but worth knowing.

For most Puerto Rican rums, mash from a previous distillation is added to the new brew, similar to the way sour mash whiskey is concocted. Aging takes place in oak casks, which may or may not be charred, depending upon the type of rum the distillers wish to produce.

The "golden" rums pick up some of their rich color from the casks in which they're aged, but most of the color comes from the addition of caramel.

Medium Rum

Here we run into a subtle distinction. While there are rum connoisseurs (there's one in every crowd) who will insist upon drinking only medium rum, the true difference between light, medium, and dark rum relates only to the individual palate.

For our home bartenders, there are two types of rum, light and dark, and myriad variations of each. Rum of either category that has been aged for approximately six years carries the distinction of being labeled *añejo*.

Dark Rum

The Caribbean island of Jamaica is synonymous with dark, full-bodied rum. Rum from such places as Guyana, also dark and heavy, is often bottled at 151 proof, great for flaming drinks (which you prepare at your peril) but also quite tasty as a sipping drink. It's called Demeraran rum. Martinique, too, produces a fine dark rum.

Most people think of rum as nothing more than an ingredient in exotic tropical drinks. That's misleading because fine rums, light or dark, can stand alone in a snifter as an after-dinner drink or predinner cocktail. As with all liquors, you'll pay top dollar for the best. But if you're willing to spring for free-range chicken for dinner at a premium price, serving your guests the best rum also makes sense. A ten-year-old rum aged in white oak, sipped neat or on the rocks, can be an absolutely magnificent drink, and Barbancourt rum, made in Haiti, is as smooth and tasty as single-barrel bourbon.

Rum was, is, and will always be a tropical drink, and so you would expect that any bar with a parrot in its name would know best what to do with it. Our two parrots, The Blue Parrot and The Green Parrot, certainly do. And Cuba's La Bodeguita del Medio, launchpad of the Mojito, is living rum history. But would you expect one of this book's great rum drinks to have been invented by an Italian gent, heralded as one of London's most celebrated barmen and perhaps the world's foremost authority on antique Cognacs?

Salvatore Calabrese, manager of The Library Bar at The Lanesborough Hotel, London, once held the same position at the famous Little Dix Bay resort on Virgin Gorda, in the British Virgin Islands. After Hurricane Marilyn blew through there in the eighties, Salvatore mixed a tribute to the destructive lady that brought the Caribbean and the United States together more smoothly than any international diplomat could ever have done.

Of course, the Mojito comes to us from La Bodeguita, Cuba, with special thanks to Sue and Alan Schoenbach, who have been educational emissaries to Cuba for some years and who have added their particular academic flair to this practical tome. The Mojito is Cuba's unofficial national cocktail, and with the recipe in this book, direct from barman Jorge Lorenzo Viqueira Lee, who shared the century-old recipe with the authors, by way of Sue and Alan, you can begin practicing in order to throw the ultimate *Fiesta del Mojito* when the wall between the United States and Cuba finally comes tumbling down.

Vicki Roush, bartender at The Green Parrot in Key West, is not enamored of folks who order frozen drinks. But when they do, she likes to knock their socks off with a Mudslide, which traditionally blends vodka, Kahlua, and Baileys. Vicki successfully uses rum instead of vodka! She makes a Tropical Mudslide with Cruzan or Mount Gay Extra Gold and a shot of crème de cocoa. If she uses Barbancourt rum from Haiti, she calls it a Haitian Mudslide. Vicki's special approach is also found in the popular recipe chapter. A friend coats a stemmed glass with Hershey's chocolate syrup prior to pouring the Mudslide—a Pennsylvania Mudslide?

Rum is a great spirit, whether it be in a Piña Colada, Zombie, Mai Tai, Daiquiri, or a simple Rum and Coke. Just don't stick one of those silly little decorative umbrellas in the tropical drinks you serve. It's your bar; set your standards high.

TEQUILA

Because many people consider tequila to be but one of many ingredients in a Margarita, they buy the cheapest brand available in their local liquor stores. That's a shame because tequila is a lovely and distinctive dry spirit on its own, best appreciated by aficionados when taken neat.

But unlike sipping an unadorned shot of great bourbon, there's a time-honored ritual to be observed when enjoying tequila this way: A shot glass is filled with tequila. A lime is cut into quarters. The imbiber rubs a lime quarter on the back of the left hand, preferably near the knuckles but most anywhere will do, and deposits a pinch of salt on the moistened area. Then, in one smooth and practiced move, the glass is grasped in the right hand, the salt licked from the back of the left hand, the tequila downed in one swallow, and the lime bitten into, the juices sucked from it as sort of a citrus chaser. As with most spirits, you get what you pay for, and that definitely includes tequila.

For a third-party endorsement of tequila's place as a premium spirit, consider what Captain Bernal Díaz, Cortez's right-hand man during Spain's conquest of Mexico, wrote in his diary back in 1521. He'd just tasted his first tequila and wrote that it was " . . . a nectar of the Aztec gods, a beverage so lovely it makes us forget fatigue and live only in a state of happiness. . . . "

Tequila versus Mezcal

Tequila is the national spirit of Mexico. A thousand or more years ago Mexicans drank *pulque*, a beerlike beverage with a low alcohol content that was made from the mezcal (agave) plant. The conquering Spaniards used their knowledge of distillation to transform pulque into tequila. They still drink *mezcal* in Mexico, but tequila bears little resemblance to that primitive beverage.

All tequila is mezcal, but not all mezcal is tequila. There are some, not many, who actually prefer mezcal to tequila. Stags Leap Winery in California has created a top-shelf mezcal called Encantado, 80 proof and double distilled. It is, according to those lucky bartenders who've managed to add a bottle to their back-bar shelves, a superb drink, especially when taken neat—smoky and earthy and easy going down. It might be worth springing a bottle on guests who request tequila, provided you can find one. (By the way, there's no worm in a bottle of Encantado, even though, contrary to popular myth, those crazy bottles with worms in them contain not tequila but mezcal.)

Tequila as we know it today is made from a plant known technically as *Agave tequilana weber,* or blue agave for short. Unlike mezcal, which is grown throughout Mexico, blue agave is found primarily in one limited geographic area, the state of Jalisco, in which the town of Tequila is located. It's a blue plant that takes anywhere from eight to twelve years to grow to maturity. When it does, its central core weighs about one hundred pounds. At maturity, the sharp spiny leaves are removed, and the core is steamed to extract the sap, or sugar. It's then allowed to ferment and is finally distilled. The result is a fresh batch of ordinary tequila ready for drinking in its "white" state. Or, it can be aged in oak barrels to give it a gold color and to soak up the flavor imparted by the oak. Aged tequila, *añejo,* produces the high end of the spirit line.

Mexican law says that tequila can be manufactured using sources of sugar other than blue agave (usually molasses) and legally still be called tequila as long as the agave accounts for at least 51 percent of sugars used. The high-end tequilas go beyond the law: They use pure agave sugar and only that from selected plants. As far as aging is concerned, according to Mexican law, *tequila añejo* must be aged at least one year in white oak casks.

Tequila's popularity has grown impressively over the past ten years, almost 25 percent, due to a large extent, no doubt, to the increasing number of Margarita lovers worldwide.

It was inevitable that some distiller would latch on to the single-barrel bourbon and single-malt Scotch craze, and develop a single-barrel tequila. Called Porfidio, it is bottled directly from the barrel with minimum filtration and no blending, and features hand-blown bottles with a glass cactus poking up attractively from the bottom. You'll pay about $60 per bottle, but your tequila-loving guests will be dutifully impressed. You can pay even more, as much as $75 a bottle, for Cuervo Reserva de la Familia, marketed by a company generally considered a mass-marketer of tequilas, Jose Cuervo.

BRANDY

Writing briefly about brandies is like writing briefly about football players: Some are huge and tough; some are sleek and fast. Some overpower you; some finesse you. And in both cases you'll want some information before tackling a player or choosing a brandy for your home bar. Here's a scouting report on brandy. You're on your own with football.

Some brandies, but not all, are cognacs; others, but not the rest, are armagnacs. Pure brandies are made from grapes; others distilled from fruits. Some make the Hall of Fame; other brandies are bench warmers—serviceable but not very exciting.

Having sniffed and sipped cognacs from the personal cellars of Napoleon and Thomas Jefferson with Salvatore Calabrese, it is difficult for us to write about metaxa in the same sentence. Having knocked back more than our share of metaxa with college roommates, it is difficult to admit that we allowed antique cognacs to pass the same palate. So, having fessed up to both polar extremities, perhaps we can proceed with empirical authority enough to keep this report on brandy balanced.

When serving a fine cognac or armagnac, or any quality brandy for that matter, a good rule of thumb is that preached by Salvatore, who has poured ounces of liquid gold valued as much as a thousand dollars a glass: Two snifters of good brandy at one sitting are enough. Anything more than that, you're wasting the experience.

There are those who argue that no cognac or armagnac should be sullied by mixing. We're inclined to agree. Fine cognacs and armagnacs should be sensated so gradually and deeply that your olfactory glands are titillated, practically to the point of hearing: "*Voilà!*" Well, at least, "Great brandy!"

Cognac

Cognac is the finest of brandies, made from the grapes of the Cognac region of France, which are crushed and double distilled. Aged in French oak, cognac's qualities are determined by the grapes used— Grande Champagne, Petite Champagne, Borderies, Fins Bois, Bois Ordinaires, Bois Terroir—and the aging process. The results appear on the label of each bottle, indicating the quality of your purchase.

The code is:

"V" for Very

"S" for Special

"O" for Old

"P" for Pale

"F" for Fine

"X" for Extra

The government of France regulates the age of Cognacs, maintaining that the words *Extra, Napoleon,* or *Vielle Reserve* qualify the contents as having been aged at least five years in oak, a reliable indicator for the home bartender.

If you're ever tempted to take a cognac lightly, remember that Winston Churchill and Dwight Eisenhower plotted the allies' victory in World War II over an 1858 Croizet that had been secreted out of France by the French underground.

Armagnac

Little sister armagnac (and those of us who have ever had one know never to take a little sister lightly) can be made from the grapes of any or all of three regions of France: Bas-Armagnac, Haut-Armagnac, and Tenareze. For some, it tantalizes where cognac teases, satisfies rather than mystifies. Each can be enjoyed in its own setting.

Beyond the two classics, brandies get fruitier and less controlled the farther from France they are produced, though by law American brandies must be aged in oak at least two years.

Other Brandies

Pre-biblical distillation of brandy from fruit likely originated in Egypt, found its way to Spain via the Moors, and spread to California by way of the Spanish missionaries. Seeds planted in fertile soil grow deep and flourish, even when transported across oceans.

Metaxa is made in Greece from a grape base. In Italy, grappas are grape-based as well but vary in quality and deadliness. Kirsch is a cherry brandy from Germany and Austria, and Calvados, from France, is derived from apples.

Whether, cherry-, apple-, or apricot-flavored, brandies should be grape-based. Otherwise they are fruit-flavored liqueurs and should be priced down accordingly. It pays to read the label. But it also pays to know in advance the purpose to which you plan to put your spirits. Fruit liqueurs belong in a punch. A good cognac belongs in a snifter, all by itself.

APÉRITIFS

The word *apéritif* was derived from the Latin word *aperire*, which means "to open," and has been liberally interpreted to mean "to open the appetite." So, an apéritif literally could be a glass of beer before dinner. Right?

"Literally, but not technically," according to Meaghan Jones of The Bar at Morton's Midtown. Technically, an apéritif is a fortified wine or aromatic wine, preferably dry, that is used to complement hors d'oeuvres and lead comfortably to a wine-accompanied dinner. It is not overpowering and, hence, tends to slide you into the evening, working more subtly than a spirit-based cocktail.

Sherry and Port are the classics, and in Europe dry or sweet vermouth serve as apéritifs. A bitter, such as Campari, with soda to temper it, is a standard, and in France quinine is added to Dubonnet. On the sweeter side, Lillet is a popular alternative in the land of the grape.

Spain is the traditional producer of sherry. Popular Spanish sherries include Dry Sack, Domecq, Harvey's of Bristol, and Emilio Lustau. After the wine is fermented, it is fortified with brandy and fermented again with yeast to make sherry. Much of sherry's flavor is derived from the casks in which it is fermented.

Dry Sack is appropriately named, in that this particular sherry was originally called "sack" and was referred to as such by none other than William Shakespeare in Henry IV, Part Two. Our favorite apéritif cocktail is the Negroni, a mix of equal parts gin, Campari, and either dry or sweet vermouth. Salvatore Calabrese of the Library Bar at London's Lanesborough Hotel prefers sweet vermouth in his Negroni, and he is not averse to a splash of soda.

CORDIALS AND LIQUEURS

Used interchangeably in the United States, these two terms denote a category of sweetened distilled spirits that was first created in the Middle Ages by alchemists in search of cure-alls. Little wonder that they are still used as a *digestif*, an aid to digestion, taken after a meal.

The roots for both words are Latin and reveal the original intent of the alchemists and the methods they used. *Cor* means "heart," suggesting the curative purpose of the cordial, and *liquefacere* means "to dissolve." To make liqueurs, sugar is dissolved in distilled spirits by distillation, percolation, maceration, or infusion. Distilling extracts the flavors by heat; percolation works just like a coffeepot, with the spirit below bubbled up over the herbs, which rest in a filter above; in maceration, the fruits are steeped in the spirit; and in infusion, they are steeped in a heated spirit.

Flavorings include herbs, flowers, spices, seeds, orange, and a variety of other fruits, which are added to spirits to create such syrupy cordials as sambuca, crème de cacao, Triple Sec, amaretto, anisette, crème de menthe, and aquavit. Name-brand cordials include such standards as Drambuie, Cointreau, Jägermeister, Kahlua, and Grand Marnier.

Cordials can contain as much as 50 percent alcohol and 35 percent sugar—sweet enough to replace dessert. Common cordial cocktails include the Grasshopper and the Apricot Sour.

WINE

Later in the book when we offer advice on what home bartenders should include in their liquor cabinet, we suggest a simple and inexpensive way to choose which wines to have on hand: Ask your local liquor store owner. But readers of this book who consider themselves wine mavens will undoubtedly accuse the authors of having given short shrift to wine selection. Perhaps we have. Truth is, the mysterious world of wine is far too complex for us to attempt to turn our fledgling home bartenders into wine experts. It can be a worthy endeavor, however, and we encourage our readers to learn more about selecting wines.

There's no question that wines vary dramatically in taste and that allowing a good wine (even a great wine if budget allows) to wash playfully over the palate is one of life's true pleasures. But as with few other things, price and quality don't necessarily go hand in hand where wine is concerned. Nor does the fact that if a wine is from France, it will, by extension, be superior in quality and taste.

By all means devote some time to learning about wine, and pursue the great wines in your local liquor store, through wine clubs, or in the proliferation of wine bars sprouting up all over the country. Bone up on the subject through any of the dozens of excellent books devoted to wine and its appreciation, or the newspaper and magazine columns that keep readers abreast of what's new in the wine world.

Given the fact that many a good wine shop offers a 5- or 10-percent discount on even mixed cases, there's no reason not to stock a variety. And, since a number of very good wines are available for about $10 a bottle, a well-stocked wine rack that can satisfy the varying tastes of discriminating guests is well within the means of most hosts and hostesses.

The authors learned this lesson well while researching a story for *Good Housekeeping* magazine on great $10 bottles of wine with Dr. Richard Vine, one of the world's foremost authorities on the subject. (Yes, "Vine" is the name with which the good doctor was born.) Dr. Vine is Professor of Enology at Purdue University, author of the definitive 700-page textbook *Wine Appreciation*, and wine consultant to American Airlines, which regularly wins awards for the quality of its cellar in the sky. Although Dr. Vine does not own a bar, nor is he a professional bartender, we happily include his expertise in *The World's Best Bartenders' Guide*. But before we go to school with Dr. Vine, a little wine history might be in order.

Wine is as old as civilization itself. There are written records of wine being enjoyed in such places as Mesopotamia and Egypt; Greek and Roman literature is rich with references to wine. The actual route taken by wine around the world is a little fuzzy, but smart thinking has it traveling from Babylon to Egypt and then to Greece and Rome. The Romans, never shy about expanding their empire, brought along the vines when they imposed themselves on France, Germany, and Spain. It was later that the vines, and skills in wine making, reached the shores of America, Africa, and Australia.

European fossils indicate that vines have been around for more than a few years before Christ, about 50 million years, in fact. Dr. Vine informs us that the most basic wines were made about 100,000 years ago, and Neolithic man drank wines with his meals at least 8,000 years ago.

The genesis of wine may literally be found in the Bible; namely Genesis 9:20–21: "And Noah began to be an husbandman, and he planted a vineyard: And he drank of the wine, and was drunken . . . " There is many a reference to wine in the Bible, perhaps the most famous that of the wedding feast at Cana in Galilee, when Jesus changed water into wine. The message, and the Bible, have lasted through the ages: Drinking wine is okay; getting drunk isn't.

Truth is, the only truly relevant wine history goes back about a hundred years. The reason for this is that prior to that point, virtually all of Europe's vines had been decimated by a disease known as *Phylloxera vitifoliae*, an invasion of vine-eating lice. Brought to the rescue, vine roots from California were exported all over the world. Onto these roots, growers in other countries grafted their own various varieties of grapes.

The relative quality of wines depends upon many factors, the most important of which are the weather and soil. Too much hot sun tends to dry out the pulp; too much rain will produce a minor crop characterized by tasteless grapes; heat can wipe out an entire crop; and a badly timed frost can be equally destructive. Soil too rich in nitrogen or potassium results in heavy vegetation but fewer grapes. All of which is why some years are considered to have produced great vintages, while others pale in comparison.

In general, southern regions are more abundant producers of wine, but those on the northern rim of such regions turn out wine that is usually more subtle and delicate.

Wine Making

Once the grapes are perfectly ripe and have been picked, they're brought to the pressing cellar, where the "vinification" process begins. Depending upon the type of wine the "vintner" wishes to produce from the grapes, he or she will press the grapes—skin, pips, stems, and all—for red wine, process just the juice for white wine, or work a carefully considered combination of both for a naturally pink, or rosé, wine.

The grapes' natural sugar, when combined with yeast, produces the fermented juice, which is aged in casks. It's a very hands-on process, no computers involved. The length of time a wine is aged, the additives used, the amount of exposure to the air, and a dozen other intangible factors determine when a wine is ready for bottling. Even then, some wines aren't really ready for consumption. These are referred to as wines for "laying down," to be stored until the natural aging process is completed in the bottle.

Storing and Serving Wine

A few words about the storing and serving of wine. Ideally, wine should be stored in a dark place where the temperature ranges from 50° to 55° Fahrenheit. They can be stored on their sides in anything as informal as an old dresser or as exotic as a commercial storage unit in which temperature, humidity, and light are controlled at a cost of thousands of dollars. We like to look at our wines and figure that if you buy bottles that have to be hermetically sealed, you've already wasted some of your money.

Bottles should never be stored standing up. Instead, they should be placed on their sides to allow the cork to remain moist. Better yet, if possible, store them standing upside down, which is not always easy, considering that virtually all wine racks are constructed for bottles to rest horizontally.

A tip concerning temperature: It's better to store a bottle of wine in a constant, room-temperature environment than to expose it to wide temperature swings. Even if the place where you store wine is on a counter in your kitchen, it's perfectly acceptable to refer to your "wine cellar." Makes sense—how many city apartments have real cellars?

Red wine should be served at cool room temperature, and should be uncorked a half hour before serving to allow it to "breathe." White wine should be slightly chilled; a half hour in the refrigerator before serving is sufficient. If you're serving white wine in an ice bucket and the wine in the bottle's neck isn't chilled enough, turn the bottle upside down.

Now, on to the wine wisdom of Dr. Vine.

There are several common mixed drinks for which wine forms the alcoholic base, such as Spritzers, Coolers, and Sangria, and you'll find these later in the book. For now, we'll head to the cellar for a look at wine in its classic varieties and pick out several for our home bar, with a tip of the hat to Dr. Vine for his insight—and his course notes.

One good thing to know when tasting wines is that they have distinctive flavors that can be identified on the palate. A bit of pleasant research can uncover plummy, oaky, buttery, cherry, berry, or any of a number of tastes. The one thing you don't want to taste is vinegar; it means your wine is turning or has already turned bad.

Let's take a quick, cribbing look at Dick Vine's study notes to find out what's behind the label of all those bottles of whites and reds.

White Wines

When aged in oak barrels or casks, white wines assimilate various intensities of toasty vanilla flavor.

Chardonnay (shar-doh-NAY)

Made from a classic grape native to the Burgundy region in France, known for its dry (not sweet) white wines with olive, fig, and earthy applelike tones of bouquet and taste. It often has a rich buttery flavor.

Johannisberg Riesling (yoh-HAH-nihs-berg REES-ling)

A classic grape from the famous German Rheinland, it is made into dry wines as well as wines with varying levels of sweetness. The sweetest types are from overripened grapes purposely allowed to decompose. The wines typically have pronounced floral-apricot flavors.

Gewürztraminer (guh-VURTZ-trah-mee-ner)

Gewürz means "spicy" in German, and this wine has a distinctive spicy-peach character that is usually semisweet. While it is native to northern Italy, its fame comes from the Alsace region of France, where it is grown.

Sauvignon Blanc (SOH-vee-yohn BLAHN)

A classic grape of the Loire Valley region in France, it is widely known for its smoky bouquet and is often referred to as *fumé*. It is usually characterized by citrus and grasslike flavors.

Semillon (say-mee-YOHN)

A famous grape native to the Bordeaux region of France, it is used for sweet wines like the Rieslings. Its flavor is rather pearlike in the dry wines and raisinlike in the sweet versions.

Red Wines

Most reds (except Gamay) are extensively aged in oak and assimilate various intensities of woody vanilla flavor.

Cabernet Sauvignon (ka-bair-NAY SOH-vee-yohn)

A classic red grape (probably native to northern Spain) that is widely cultivated in the Bordeaux chateau region of France. The wine has a dense scarlet color and is dry, with flavors characterized as black currant, cedar, and green pepper.

Gamay (gaah-MAY)

A famous grape of the Beaujolais district of Burgundy, it produces a medium, ruby-red dry wine that has a distinctive cherry flavor.

Merlot (mer-LOH)

Also identified with Bordeaux, it is a close cousin of Cabernet Sauvignon, with a somewhat softer acidity and less intense flavor. A bit more "berryish."

Pinot Noir (PEE-noh NWAHR)

A classic grape of the Burgundy and Champagne regions of France. As a Burgundy, it is a light, brick-red, dry wine, with briar and coffee flavors. As a Champagne, it is a light, earthy-flinty white sparkling wine.

BEER

Beer drinking has come a long way in terms of sophistication since the days when you bought a six-pack of whatever domestic beer was on sale and drank it without paying much attention to its flavor. Today, with the burgeoning number of brands, choosing and savoring a glass of beer is akin to tasting and appreciating a particular wine.

It's impossible to pinpoint how many beers there are; estimates range from twenty to thirty thousand. Beer is produced in virtually every country of the world, and its importation to the United States has resulted in myriad choices for American beer lovers.

In a sense, beer is the forerunner of whiskey, which, after all, starts with a beer that is then distilled. A perusal of history indicates that the Egyptians were brewing beer as much as 6,500 years ago, maybe even earlier. Beer allowed those living in climates not conducive to grape growing to produce an alcoholic beverage. As long as grain was available, it was possible to create beer. Beer, in its simplest terms, is nothing more than malted grain fermented with yeast and flavored with various hops.

Hops, one of the factors that gives each beer its distinctive flavor (along with the yeast used, the fermentation process, the local water, the skill of the brewer, and the strength and quality of the malt), are the dried, ripe flowers of the hop vine. Their oil, which is bitter and aromatic, is what gives beer its distinctive sharp taste. Hops also help preserve beer by preventing bacterial growth.

But it wasn't until the fifteenth century that hops were introduced as a flavor-enhancer into the beer-making process, most likely by the Dutch. And it was this country's earliest settlers, the Pilgrims, who brought the knowledge of making beer to these shores, brewing it in their own homes. The first sizable commercial brewery was established in Pennsylvania by that state's founding father, William Penn.

The production of the more familiar brands, Budweiser, Miller, etc., is very much an assembly-line procedure. But the booming microbrewery industry in America is grounded in eschewing mass production and returning to a more hands-on approach, which has resulted in beers with highly individualistic character and taste. Many beers produced abroad also have many of the features of microbrewing.

Like wine, cigars, books, and recordings, different beers can be sampled through Beer-of-the-Month clubs. It's a good way to enjoy a variety of brews, some of which will please you to the extent that you'll stock them in your home bar.

And if you really want to put a personal stamp on the beer you serve guests, brew your own at home or, better yet, take advantage of "U-brews," small do-it-yourself breweries sprouting up in various cities at which home bartenders can utilize state-of-the-art brewing equipment, receive expert instruction, and, when the brewing is done, return to bottle and custom-label his or her creations.

The making of all beers follows a series of basic steps, but it is the variations introduced by each brewer that results in the general categories into which beer types fall. There are two basic types of beer—ale and lager.

Ale

When yeast is added during the brewing process to ferment beer, the choice is to allow it to ferment on top of the "wort" (the liquid) or on the bottom. Beers classified as ale are fermented on top, which produces a slightly more alcoholic beer than lager, which is bottom fermented.

Types of Ale

Bitter

A light ale containing a hefty dose of hops, giving it a bitter taste and its name.

Stout

This is the "black beer" that's become so popular in this country. It gains its color and sharp flavor from the introduction of roasted barley during the brewing process.

Porter

Another dark beer, less alcoholic than stout, which gains its flavor from the dark malts used in its processing. Originally created in England as a lower-priced beer for servants (hall porters liked it, giving it its name), it has what could almost be called a flavor not unlike coffee.

Pale

This is a light-colored ale that's made with less hops than bitter.

Brown

Another variety of dark ale, which tastes sweeter than pale ale.

Lager

Drink a can of American mass-produced beer and you're drinking a lager, which was the original German way of brewing. (*Lager* is the German word for "storehouse.") Lagers are lighter in flavor and body than ales.

Bock (or Boch)

This is a dark lager, containing more potent malts and a higher percentage of sugar. The symbol for bock beer is a goat's head, believed to have come from the Hindu word *bokra*, which translates as "billygoat."

Pilsner

A light, dry lager originally brewed in Pilzen, Czechoslovakia, which has become the prototype for America's most popular beers.

Malt Liquor

Malt liquor is the term applied to any beer that exceeds a state's maximum alcohol content.

WHAT THE
HOME BARTENDER
NEEDS

Ahome being one's castle, as is said, it follows that the level of entertaining that takes place there is highly individualistic. Being invited for dinner at one person's home might involve the simplest of meals; at another, only the most elegant of offerings.

Every skilled chef has a few signature dishes that he or she has thoroughly tested on family members before serving to guests. Home bartenders, too, are wise to develop some signature drinks whose preparation has been perfected. These can be either a few of the most popular drinks, perhaps customized by the home bartender, or original creations. In either case, practice does, indeed, make perfect.

Our professional bartenders have their specialty drinks, too. At the same time, they're prepared to fulfill hundreds of customer requests, most of which they've committed to memory. Even so, they're never too proud to consult a bartenders' guide when faced with a request unfamiliar to them.

The question for the home bartender is whether to offer guests a limited menu of drinks, or to learn the craft and art of drink making to the extent that a wide variety of drink orders can be filled. Our professional bartenders differ somewhat in regard to this. A few suggest learning to make a few drinks well and offering only those to guests. But the majority urge home bartenders to become adept at mixing as many drinks as possible; in other words, to become skilled and "professional" behind your home bar.

We have friends who prepare a printed drink menu on their computers to hand to guests upon their arrival. On it they list the types of spirits available, choices of mixed drinks for the evening, wines, varieties of beer on ice, and soft drinks. It's a nice approach, if only to make guests' selections a little easier.

Other friends take the "less is more" approach and choose one or two drinks to serve on a given evening and limit their guests' choices to them. In some cases only wine will be served. In others, a punch is what's available before dinner.

The authors find the single-drink approach to entertaining to be unnecessarily restrictive. For us, guests should be able to enjoy the cocktail of their choice before dinner, with obvious limitations.

The single-choice concept does work, however, when it is linked to a particular event or season. A Mexican meal might be preceded only by Margaritas, or a German feast by imported German beer. A house full of guests from Boston could justify a round of Ward Eights. Similarly, the New Orleans side of the family might enjoy Sazerac cocktails. There is a potential danger, of course, in serving drinks that are synonymous with a certain city or bar. Guests from those places are used to the "real thing." Follow the directions carefully in this book and practice before going into competition with Boston's Locke-Ober bar, where the Ward Eight was introduced, or the Sazerac Bar at New Orleans' Fairmont Hotel.

A cozy January evening in front of a roaring fire is certainly justification for featuring a hot alcoholic beverage, just as a scorchingly hot summer day is reason for whipping up and serving one of the special Caribbean cocktails featured in *The World's Best Bartenders' Guide*.

But, in general, it's the authors' intention to inspire as well as to help prepare every home bartender to be a professional in his or her own home, to take pride in what's available for guests from their home bars, and to cause the New Orleans contingent to proclaim at the end of the evening, "That's the best Sazerac cocktail I've ever had, even better than the ones served at The Fairmont Hotel."

Although the drink recipes in this book number into the hundreds, the majority of them are made by skillfully blending just a few basic ingredients. The extent to which you go to stock and equip your home bar will depend upon how ambitious you are, your budget, and space. But no matter how ambitious your intentions, preparation is a key factor, just as it is when planning an elaborate meal.

Manuel "Mannix" Ramírez, fifteen years at the bar of the lovely Casa de Sierra Nevada in San Miguel de Allende, Mexico, preaches preparation for any bartender, professional or home-style: "They [bartenders] should present a cocktail to a guest as though it is a special present. They need to check their bars in advance to make sure they'll have everything needed . . . [when guests arrive]."

STOCKING THE BAR

Stocking Liquors

Here's what liquors any well-stocked home bar should contain. And remember, the few extra dollars it costs to buy the best will pay off in contented guests who don't complain about the evening on the way home, provided, of course, that the conversation was as palatable as the food and drink.

Blended American whiskey

Blended bourbon (for mixed bourbon drinks)

Blended Scotch (for mixed drinks)

Brandy and cognac

Canadian whisky

Citrus-flavored vodkas (perhaps lemon and orange)

Gin

Irish whiskey

Pepper vodka

Rum (both light and dark, preferably añejo)

Single-barrel bourbon (for drinking neat)

Single-malt Scotch (for sipping)

Tequila (both white and gold)

Vermouth (both sweet and dry)

Vodka (good-quality plain Russian)

For someone just beginning to build and stock a home bar, this list might seem to represent a substantial outlay of money. It is. But bear in mind that once the bar is properly stocked, most bottles will last a long time, needing to be replenished only occasionally.

Stocking Other Liquors and Liqueurs

There are other liquors and liqueurs that round out a well-stocked home bar. Certain recipes that capture your fancy will necessitate adding some of these to your shelves. They are:

Amaretto

Anisette

Applejack or Calvados

Armagnac

Baileys Irish Cream

B & B

Benedictine

Campari

Chambord

Chartreuse (green and yellow)

Cointreau or Triple Sec

Crème de banane

Crème de cacao (light and dark)

Crème de cassis

Crème de menthe (white and green)

Crème de noyeaux

Drambuie

Dubonnet (white and red)

Framboise

Frangelico

Fruit-flavored brandies

Galliano

Grand Marnier

Grappa

Irish Mist

Kahlua

Kirsch

Kirschwasser

Lillet

Maraschino liqueur

Midori

Pernod

Pimm's Cup

Rock 'n' Rye

Sambuca (white or black)

Schnapps (peach and/or peppermint)

Sloe Gin

Southern Comfort

Strega

Tia Maria

Tuaca

Vandermint

There are others, of course. If you do purchase any of these supplements to your basic bar stock because you intend to make a drink calling for them in the mix, buy the smallest bottle possible.

Many home bars will be an available kitchen counter; others will consist of a "real" bar, with a serving counter, perhaps a few stools, and back-bar shelving on which bottles of spirits are displayed. The latter is obviously preferable not only because it creates a more efficient area in which to concentrate on making drinks, but also because it looks great. A few shelves on which inviting bottles of premium liquors are proudly displayed, the spotless bottles (you will, of course, see that they're spotless before guests arrive) glistening in lights behind the bar, set a wonderful visual tone. Our professional bartenders make a point of reminding bartenders of the home variety that the serving of drinks involves a certain element of show business. Just as you set your dinner table with your best china and linens, gently burning fresh candles, and gleaming glassware, you should also provide an attractive setting in which to serve drinks.

Stocking Wine

Naturally, you'll want to have on hand a selection of red and white wines. You'll note that we've included such wine-based products as Dubonnet, vermouth, and Lillet in the section above. Although they technically fall under the wine umbrella, they are used in cocktails more often than served alone in a wine glass.

Individual taste will determine which wines to include in your home bar's inventory. A good way to go about this is to buy a mixed case of wines in the following two categories:

Dry reds (such as Cabernet Sauvignon or Merlot)

Dry white (such as a Chardonnay)

Liquor stores will often give a discount for mixed cases, generally 10 percent. If your local liquor store owner seems to possess a fairly decent wine IQ, let him or her choose the labels to be included in the case. Sample them at your leisure at home, and focus on two or three that especially please your palate. Then, stock up on those labels to form the basis of your wine rack.

You should consider adding to your stock a bottle each of tawny Port, dry sherry, rosé, and a few bottles of dry, or "brut," Champagne.

Suffice it to say that there are available many excellent moderately priced wines that will provide your guests with a pleasant drink to sip predinner and to accompany your kitchen's culinary efforts.

Thus forearmed, let's make a selection, so that when your guest asks, "Have you got a Chardonnay?" you can answer, "My dear, I have a Chardonnay just for you!" Let's start with a Chardonnay that's a terrific buy (we've seen it in shops priced from $5.99 to $9.99). Columbia Crest Chardonnay has a distinctive oaky flavor that nicely complements Edam or Gouda cheeses as well as a roast chicken. Columbia Crest, located in the state of Washington, also makes a hearty Cabernet Sauvignon (about $10) and a smooth Merlot (about $12). No home wine cellar should be without all three. Washington State also is home to the Paul Thomas Winery, which produces a good Chardonnay for about $10.

J. Lohr creates a magnificent buttery Chardonnay for about $12, as does Rodney Strong, both from California. *Wine Spectator* magazine named Forest Glen Chardonnay one of the one-hundred best wines in the world, and it costs only about ten bucks. Fetzer makes a good Chardonnay for about $7 and a very good dry Cabernet for about $8.

Dr. Vine says the best Merlot for the money in the United States is Wente Brothers, a perfect match for a grilled sirloin. Our picks for an under-$10 Gewürztraminer and a Riesling are Geyser Peak Gewürztraminer and Argyle Dry Riesling from Oregon. One of the finest American dry Rieslings we've ever tasted was produced by a couple of Czechoslovakian brothers who fled their country just before the Soviets moved in, started a construction business in eastern Pennsylvania, and in every spare moment turned some seventy acres, over twenty years, into a superb vineyard. It sells for about $15, but it's worth more, and it's called Johannisberg Riesling Private Reserve from the Sand Castle Winery. Try to get a case of the 1991 or 1992 vintage. Sand Castle's Private Reserve Chardonnay also is excellent. These folks are about to put the Delaware River valley on the wine-making map.

From Australia, you can always trust Rosemount Estate, particularly if there's a Cabernet Sauvignon label on the bottle as well as a price tag of around $11. Also from Australia, Lindeman's Chardonnay, which costs about $10, has proven to be very popular in the United States. And from the land down under, try anything from Jacob's Creek or Black Opel for some fruity flavors. Dr. Vine recommends Penfolds Chardonnay for about $12 and Koonunga Hill Cabernet/Shiraz for about $11.

One of the greatest Chardonnay buys in any wine shop is Concha y Toro from Chile. It has an oaky flavor and sells for between $7 and $9 for a 1.5-liter (magnum) bottle. Concha y Toro also offers up a tasty Cabernet Sauvignon and a mellow Merlot as well as a blend of the two, all great buys at less than $10 per magnum. If you're a California loyalist, a magnum of good Country Cabernet Sauvignon by August Sebastiani can be had for $10.

Moving over to our Pinot Noir rack, we find a lot of bottles but only one label: Napa Ridge. There are two reasons for this exclusivity. We like to buy it by the case for $7 a bottle, and Dick Vine says it's the best wine buy in America.

Moving on to good buys from France, we find a 1993 Paul Buisse Chinon Vielli Sous Bois, which sells for about $16, and a Bour Gueil Cabernet and a Vielli Sous Bois, both for about $14.

If you want to try a really good French blend without paying for a big Bordeaux, try a 1990 Château Saint Sulpice for about $12. It's 60 percent Merlot, 40 percent Cabernet. And if you want to impress without taking out a second mortgage, try a second label from Bordeaux. Second labels are from young vineyards, which are just slightly lower in quality than the first label but a fraction of the price. For instance, either a 1989 Château Lafite Rothschild Carraudes Pauillac or a 1989 Pavillon Rouge Château Margaux can be had for between $30 and $35. Uncork one of these for your significant other, boss, or client, and the evening is yours.

Domaine St. Michelle is a good-value, not-pricey sparkling wine, as is Rotari Brut from Italy, both for a little over $10. Somewhat pricey, but worth every penny, two of our favorite Champagnes are Perrier-Jouet and Veuve Clicquot Ponsardin, both around $30 per bottle.

Clifton Fadiman, one of the literary world's more erudite gentlemen, once commented, "To take wine into our mouths is to savor a droplet of the river of human history." Or, for a slightly less erudite evaluation from the authors of *The World's Best Bartenders' Guide*, "Drinking wine is fun."

Stocking Beer

Beer drinkers were once considered at the low end of the food chain—guys with muscles who popped open a can and swigged it down, then reached for another. Unfortunately, that negative stereotype still exists to some extent, unfortunate because today's beer drinkers can be as sophisticated in their taste as any lover of fine wines. This has come about, in part, because of the remarkable proliferation of microbrewery products. More than 300 new microbreweries were opened in 1996, making a total of 1,300 by year's end. Supply has truly met demand. The beer-drinking public has demanded a wide variety of beers from which to choose; these small, regional, even local breweries have met the challenge.

A casual visit to any beverage supply company tells the tale better than we can. There are literally hundreds of beers from which to choose, each possessing the unique characteristics of the area in which it was brewed, including imports from every corner of the earth. What should you choose to have on-hand when preparing for a houseful of guests?

Like wine, it pays to taste a few beers yourself before deciding. You can't go wrong by stocking an assortment from which your guests can choose. This is a good reason to prepare a printed bar menu to hand your guests when they arrive. On it you can list the beers available to them rather than have to recite the list to each new arrival.

Have on hand:

A "regular" beer (Budweiser, Coors, Miller, etc.)

An imported beer

A lite beer

A nonalcoholic beer

A sampling of popular microbrewery beers

Whichever you choose, remember that the proper serving of any beer demands that it be icy cold and served in a chilled or frosted mug or Pilsner glass.

One of the classiest home bars the authors have enjoyed visiting features beer on tap. Sam Davis, a business and financial advisor in North Salem, New York, and his wife, Marcia, purchased the professional unit made by Beverage-Air back in 1974 and have kept it in constant use ever since. Sam uses the unit to dispense a variety of beers, kegs purchased from his local beverage supply store. His only caveat is that he will not install a keg unless the store can also provide the appropriate "marker," or screw-on top, indicating what sort of beer is being served.

"There are many advantages to enjoying tap beer at home," Sam says. "It's easy to enjoy a half glass instead of having to open a whole bottle. The last glass tastes as good as the first. It's more cost-effective than serving bottles or cans. But, most important, it tastes a lot better from the tap."

Sam's Beverage-Air unit cost him approximately $600 back in 1974. Obviously, it costs considerably more today. But it's probably worth it to see the look of pleasant surprise on the faces of guests when they're offered tap beer in the home, and their enjoyment of its superior taste.

Mixers

Unless you have a house filled with guests wanting only to sip premium liquors neat, without anything else in the glass (except, perhaps, ice), you'll need the appropriate mixers and condiments with which to create perfectly mixed drinks.

A word of advice: Buy *small* bottles of mixers. Once opened, they go flat and/or they go bad. If you do have some leftovers and aren't planning another party in the next few days, empty the bottles down the drain and start fresh with your next guests. Morton's barman Sean McCarthy puts it this way: "People buy a liter of tonic. You're not going to serve a liter of tonic water, and it will sit there for six months. Buy six-ounce bottles."

Unlike the foregoing list of "Other Liquors and Liqueurs," from which one or two might be purchased to fulfill the needs of a particular mixed drink for a particular party, these basic mixers should always be available in the properly stocked home bar.

Basic Mixers

Bottled water

Club soda

Cola

Diet cola

Fresh lemon and lime juice (preferably the lemons and limes
from which to juice on the spot)

Ginger ale

Grapefruit juice

Milk

Orange juice

Rose's lime juice (it's sweet; not to be substituted for regular
lime juice)

Tomato juice

Tonic water

To that list can be added the following optional mixers, if you've
decided to follow a specific drink recipe calling for them.

Optional Mixers

Beef bouillon

Clamato juice

Coffee

Cranberry juice

Cream of coconut

Ginger beer

Lemonade

Pineapple juice

Peach nectar

Raspberry syrup

Sweet-and-sour

Of course, you might go on to develop your own mixed drinks, calling for something not on these lists. Go for it, and add the extra ingredients to your bar shopping list.

Basic Condiments/Ingredients

Besides mixers, many drinks call for condiments and garnishes, which are vitally important if a drink is to taste, and look, the way guests expect it to. It's in the use of condiments and garnishes that individual discretion can be exercised by any bartender, although as in music, where it's necessary to learn the basic melody before being able to effectively improvise on the tune, the home bartender should learn to make drinks in the classic way, following the recipe, before becoming adventuresome in the use of condiments.

Angostura bitters

Black pepper (coarsely ground with a good mill)

Celery

Cinnamon

Cocktail olives

Cocktail onions

Fresh fruit (strawberries, blueberries, etc., for select tropical
    drinks)

Grenadine

Horseradish

Maraschino cherries

Salt (regular and coarse)

Sugar (superfine)

Tabasco sauce

Worcestershire sauce

Sugar

A word about sugar: Few recipes call for the use of granulated sugar. Whenever a recipe in *The World's Best Bartenders' Guide* calls for sugar, we mean superfine sugar, which dissolves almost instantly, unless another sugar is called for in a specific recipe. Your guests should only taste sugar's sweetness, never feel it on their teeth in granular form.

If you don't wish to buy superfine sugar, do what many of our pros do: make a sugar syrup. It's easy. Mix a pound of granulated sugar with 2 cups of water in a saucepan and bring it to a boil. Let it simmer for ten to fifteen minutes, stirring often. When it's cool, pour the mixture into a bottle and keep it in the refrigerator.

Bitters

The most popular bitter for use in drinks is Angostura, a product of Trinidad. Another one called for by some recipes is Peychaud's, New Orleans's gift to the world of bitters, the product of herbs, roots, and berries. And there's Orange Bitters, from England.

They all taste the way their basic name implies: They're bitter and are used in extremely small amounts in drinks. A dash (about an eighth of a teaspoon) will generally do. One of our professional bartenders recalls a customer ordering shot glasses of Angostura, and downing them one after another, perhaps because he thought he wasn't drinking an alcoholic beverage. Bitters do contain a small amount of alcohol and shouldn't be served in any fashion to guests who can't tolerate alcohol.

BAR EQUIPMENT

As any carpenter knows, having the proper tools makes a job easier and makes it generally come out better. The same holds true for bartending. Of course, our professionals enjoy working behind elaborately stocked and equipped bars, paid for by their establishments' owners. But the home bartender can equip a home bar quite nicely, without spending a fortune.

We've already mentioned (and urged) the purchase of premium spirits. The same holds true for a few select pieces of bar equipment. Although aluminum is cheaper than stainless steel, don't buy aluminum utensils for your professionally inspired home bar. Any acidic liquid will compromise aluminum, resulting in a metallic taste in the drinks made with them. Stick to stainless steel and glass only!

Here are some of the utensils (and gadgets) you should consider purchasing for your home bar:

Bar Spoon Not just any old spoon will do. The classic bar spoon used by our professionals has a flat head, and its shaft is twisted, which helps when making Pousse-Cafés. Also, the spoon is extra long for mixing drinks in a deep mixing glass.

Bar Towels *Clean* dish towels.

Blender A blender is a must for any home bar, particularly in summer, when frozen drinks are in vogue. The blender you buy will depend upon your budget, but the stronger the motor, the more easily it will grind ice.

Bottle Opener and Can Opener Opt for one that functions to both open bottles and puncture cans.

Citrus Reamer The old-fashioned glass variety will do quite nicely for extracting the juice of oranges, lemons, and limes. Our professional bartenders all insist upon using freshly squeezed juices, and you should, too. "Massage" the fruit on a counter before using the reamer. It softens the pulp and allows the juice to flow more freely.

Coil-Rimmed Strainer The coil fits neatly into the shaker's metal portion after a drink has been shaken, enabling you to pour the drink into glasses without allowing the ice cubes to accompany it.

Corkscrew The basic model used by waiters all over the world will do nicely, unless you prefer the wing-tip version, which some people find easier to manipulate. A common problem nonprofessionals have with the waiter's corkscrew is trying to pull the cork from the bottle with too much force. Once the corkscrew is almost all the way into the cork, pull back *gently*. Another problem is not centering the corkscrew on the cork. A magnificent invention from France called the "Screwpull" corkscrew removes corks perfectly and easily every time, and the company also makes a handy foil cutter to unwrap the bottle's top.

Double-Ended Measure Ingredients in drinks should be measured, not eye-balled. Our bartenders recommend a double-ended jigger that measures 1½ ounces on one side (a jigger) and 1 ounce on the other (what's called the "pony" side).

Glass Pitcher Citrus juices and preseasoned Bloody Mary mix look attractive in a sparkling glass pitcher. Besides, it keeps those juices close at hand.

Ice Bucket and Tongs Ice buckets look good on any bar and keep ice frozen longer.

Measuring Cup A 1-cup measuring cup is essential.

Measuring Spoons One for dry ingredients; one for wet.

Mixing Glass A separate tall glass in which to stir drinks comes in handy, although you can readily use the glass portion of your shaker set for this purpose.

Muddler Not a necessity since the back of a wooden spoon, or the back of your bar spoon in the mixing glass, will do for muddling sugar and fruit or for crushing mint leaves for Mint Juleps. But having a proper muddler made of either wood or ceramic adds a nice visual touch to your bar. You'll most likely find one in a kitchen supply store.

Napkins and Coasters Often forgotten at a home bar, and so often needed.

Paring Knife Buy a good one and designate it exclusively for use at your home bar. Keep it sharp. Cutting fruit for garnishes will be easier with a keen blade.

Shaker This is sometimes referred to as a "Boston shaker"—why, we have no idea. It consists of two conical vessels with flat bottoms, one made of glass, the other of metal (stainless steel, please). The top of the glass portion fits snugly into the wider metal top, allowing for a whole lot of shaking going on when a recipe calls for such action. The glass portion also serves nicely as a tall, utilitarian bar glass in which to stir drinks, when that's appropriate.

Small Cutting Board A plastic one can go in the dishwasher for easy cleanup.

Speed Pourers Not essential, especially if you take our professional bartenders' advice and measure ingredients into a drink. But if you want to venture into the more daring aspects of bartending, pick up some speed pourers at your kitchen or restaurant supply store while purchasing your muddler. These are the tops you see on bottles in virtually every bar. The bartender holds the bottle upside down over the glass and allows the liquor to flow. Bear in mind they've done this thousands of times and know how long to hold the bottle there to dispense a precise shot. You can practice at home by filling an empty bottle with water, upending the bottle over a shot glass, and doing a count. If you do the real thing at a party and guests are watching, count silently. No sense giving away that you're new at this and aren't quite sure what you're doing. Advice: Use your speed pourers at home to amuse yourself, but measure drinks for guests with your two-headed jigger.

Straws, Swizzle Sticks, and Toothpicks Keep a variety on hand.

GLASSWARE

"Don't use gas station giveaways!" So says Eddie Doyle, who's been presiding over the bar at Boston's Bull 'n' Finch Pub, aka "Cheers," for almost twenty-five years. Robert Schwartz, popular barkeep at The Club Bar at Beverly Hills's trendy Peninsula Hotel, is equally as blunt: "Sure, you can shake a Martini using an empty Welch's grape jelly glass, but it looks lousy. Pouring an ice-cold beer into a coffee mug tastes almost the same as it does in a frosted Pilsner glass, but it looks lousy! Invest a few dollars in good glassware." Ray Bond of the bar at The Mansion on Turtle Creek in Dallas says, "The coldest Martini, the finest crafted cognac, the oldest single-malt [Scotch] will sink to below average if served in a plastic tumbler. The glassware does not have to be expensive crystal, but it must be right for the particular drink."

What Is "Good Glassware"?

For Nathan Yu, bartender at Washington, DC's lovely Library Lounge at The Carlton Hotel, it can only be French crystal by Cristal d'Arc, or Reidel crystal from Austria. But for you, the home bartender, your choice of the right glassware in which to serve your professionally inspired drinks need not be that ambitious, or expensive.

A few basic types of glasses will suffice for any home bar, each of them doing double duty. San Francisco's Top of the Mark's Andre Zotoff says, "You do not have to buy every glass imaginable. One set [each] of highball glasses, rocks glasses, wine glasses, champagne glasses, and brandy glasses is plenty." Others of our contributing bartenders suggest that home bartenders can get by with an even smaller basic array of glassware.

But if home bartenders using this book as their guide accept the premise that a home bar should be set up and operated with as much care and attention to detail as the kitchen and the dining room, buying the proper mix of glassware makes as much sense as carefully choosing place settings, tablecloths, flatware, china, candles, and, yes, glassware for the dinner table.

Before we present a consensus of our bartenders as to what glassware should be part of every home bar, it's important to point out that the various types of glasses, while visually enhancing the drinks served in them, also serve a practical purpose. There's function as well as form.

For example, a champagne "flute," with its narrow opening, was designed that way by the French to keep the bubbles inside the glass for as long as possible. We serve cocktails in "cocktail glasses" so that we grip only the stem, thereby avoiding warming the drink with heat from our hand. Conversely, we cradle a brandy "snifter" for precisely the opposite reason, to impart our hand's warmth to the brandy, which helps release its lovely aroma. And beer mugs and glasses aren't frosted only because it looks and feels nice; the chilled container keeps the brew at the proper temperature longer.

Glassware you choose to have behind your home bar will be determined, of course, by what drinks you intend to serve on any given evening. But if you wish to offer guests a wide variety of drinks, having some of each is the way to go.

And please, no colored glassware. Part of the appeal of a drink is its natural color. Clear glass only!

Recommended Glassware

Here's what glassware our fifty bartenders suggest for the home bartender.

Brandy Snifters They come in a wide range of sizes, from as small as 4 ounces to as large as 24-ounce giants. No matter what the size, the mouth of the glass should be smaller than the short, squat base to keep in the brandy's delightful aroma. Because the stem is short, the hand cups the glass itself, imparting natural warmth to the spirit contained in it.

Beer Glasses Take your choice: either a glass mug or a Pilsner glass for serving your guests beer. Either runs from 10 to 14 ounces. No matter which you choose, frost them before serving beer in them. (Some tips on this are on pages 83–84.)

Champagne Glasses Champagne can be served in a wide-mouthed glass with a stem, although our bartenders tend to favor the 6- to 10-ounce *fluted* champagne glass for reasons stated earlier.

Cocktail Glasses If you're offering Martinis or Manhattans straight up, these are the pretty glasses in which to serve them. The cocktail glass is synonymous with elegant cocktails; it's the illustration used whenever an article is about cocktails. The slender stem feels good to the hand while keeping the hand's warmth from the precious liquid in its shallow, tapered "bowl" on top.

Collins Glasses These frosted glasses, taller and slimmer than the highball glass, are available in sizes from 10 to 14 ounces and are perfect for serving Collins drinks—summer favorites with lots of ice, fruit juices, and, of course, a spirit.

Cordial Glasses Also known as "ponies," these 1-ounce glasses come in handy when serving cordials, or if you're in the mood to attempt the ultimate bartender's slight of hand, the Pousse-Café.

Highball Glasses These are your basic, tall, 8- to 12-ounce glasses in which you can serve a variety of mixed drinks, like Gin and Tonic, Rye and Ginger Ale, Scotch and Soda, or Bloody Marys.

Irish Coffee Mugs These versatile 8- to 12-ounce coffee mugs are perfect for any hot drink, including Irish Coffee or just plain ol' nonalcoholic brew.

Old-Fashioned Glasses They range in size from 4 to 10 ounces. Although these short, hefty glasses are named after a specific drink, they're a versatile addition to the home bar. Any on-the-rocks drinks are properly presented in them.

Sherry Glasses The proper type of glass, 3 to 4 ounces in size, for, of course, sherry, or other varieties of apéritifs.

Shot Glasses A 1- to 2-ounce shot glass does double duty as a serving glass for whiskey neat and as a measuring device.

Sour Glasses Sours of any variety (Scotch, bourbon, rye, or Canadian) belong in this type of glass. Like the cocktail glass, it has a stem that feels good in the hand and keeps the drink cold longer. You can buy them in sizes ranging from 4 to 6 ounces.

Wine Glasses Purists insist that there should be two different types of wine glasses behind every bar: a larger, balloon-shaped one (8 to 14 ounces) for red wine and a smaller one (6 to 8 ounces) for white. While our participating professional bartenders generally agree it's nice to have both on hand, and do behind their elaborately equipped bars, the home bartender will do quite nicely with a set of one type of wine glasses for serving both red and white. More important is the quality of the glass—and the wine.

MEASURES

Because many of the bars on our list are in countries other than America, the bartenders presented their drink recipes in metric terms. We've translated these into our language of ounces. But you may one day be given a recipe when traveling abroad. For that reason, here's a handy table of measurements for any home bartender:

MEASURE	U.S.	METRIC
Dash	$\frac{1}{32}$ oz. ($\frac{1}{8}$ teaspoon)	0.9 ml.
Splash	$\frac{1}{4}$ oz.	7.5 ml.
Teaspoon	$\frac{1}{8}$ oz.	3.7 ml.
Tablespoon	$\frac{1}{2}$ oz. (3 teaspoons)	15.0 ml.
Pony	1 oz.	30.0 ml.
Jigger	$1\frac{1}{2}$ oz.	44.5 ml.
Cup	8 oz.	257.0 ml.

TRICKS OF THE TRADE

N ow that you've pledged to become a great home bartender, and have a properly stocked and equipped home bar, it's time to pick up a few "tricks of the trade" from our professional bartenders at the "World's Fifty Greatest Bars."

Tending bar is a mental exercise. It doesn't demand much in the way of physical exertion. If you can pour from a bottle, stir a mixed drink, or shake a blended one, you've passed the physical.

SOME BASIC RULES

There are three reasons why you shouldn't give any guest too much to drink.

1. It's irresponsible. Our pros unanimously cite bar patrons who drink too much as among their least favorite customers. A good bartender has the well-being of every guest uppermost in mind, and that includes knowing when to cut someone off, particularly if driving is involved.

2. If a bartender deviates from accepted standard drink recipes in order to pour a guest "a stiff drink," the taste of the drink, whatever that drink may be, is not what it should be. In other words, you've made a lousy drink.

Patrick Negron, who makes perfect drinks of every description at Seattle's Ray's Boathouse, says, "The most common mistake I see is the person who thinks more booze makes a better drink." Or, in the words of bartender Vicki Roush at Key West's popular Green Parrot bar, "Don't overpour! Getting your guests completely whacked is not the goal of any host."

3. Either or both of the above "violations" brand the bartender a rank amateur. Be a pro. See to it that your guests enjoy drinks made by you the proper way, imbibe with moderation, and don't drive if they've been drinking.

TYPES OF DRINKS

In reality, there are only three types of drinks to be made: highballs, stirred cocktails, and shaken cocktails.

Highballs

These are drinks in which an alcoholic beverage is combined with a mixer and ice, and stirred with the long handle of a bar spoon. If the highball involves a carbonated beverage, stir gently in order to avoid dissipating too many bubbles. But you must stir, if even a few times. It thoroughly mixes the ingredients together, brings the liquids in uniform contact with the ice, and, well, it's the way professional bartenders do it.

Stirred Cocktails

These are stirred in a vessel other than the glass in which they'll be served. It fascinated the authors to learn how many pros have a set ritual when stirring is involved. Some have their timing down to perfection ("stir for precisely eighteen seconds"). Others count the number of times the stirrer moves through the drink. Still others silently say something each time they stir to ensure a perfect drink. Actually, there's a tangible reason for not stirring a cocktail for too short a time. The act of stirring dilutes the ice just enough to create the right mix of alcohol and water. Contrary to the belief of some bartenders, usually of the home variety, who are determined to not allow melting ice to dilute their drinks, the proper amount of water contributes to the perfect taste of the cocktail, even Martinis.

We present individual stirring and shaking rituals in the chapter devoted to making the most popular drinks.

Shaken Cocktails

Here, a certain manual dexterity is called for. The obvious goal, of course, is to not allow the two parts of the shaker to come apart in mid shake. Assuming you're using a classic shaker with two parts—one stainless steel, the other glass (as opposed to screwing on the top of a former mayonnaise jar)—the technique championed by our pros is to always combine the ingredients in the glass portion, then cup the metal portion over the glass. Hold the shaker at a slight angle and, using both hands, shake gently in an up-and-down motion. Not too vigorously or you'll inject too many ice shavings into the mix.

When you're finished shaking, and with the glass portion upright, tap the metal part with the heel of your hand or gently against the edge of the bar until the two pieces separate. Hold the metal vessel upright and pour the shaken drink into it. Put the coil strainer over the top of the metal container in order to keep ice from accompanying the drink, and pour into the proper glass.

Any drinks calling for the use of eggs, cream, citrus juices, thick liqueurs, or other "heavy" ingredients should be shaken with vigor. *Really* shaken!

ICE

Of all the ingredients used by professional bartenders, *ice* seems to be the dominant topic of their advice for the home bartender. Here's a sampling of some of their comments:

"Get lotsa ice!" Robert Brady, The Capital Grille, Chicago.

"Lots of ice!" Bob Sorenson, The Pump Room, Chicago.

"Plenty of ice!" Sean Boyd, The Horseshoe Bar, Dublin, Ireland.

"Don't run out of ice!" Liz Cape, Club Lucky, Toronto, Canada.

The consensus is that if a drink is supposed to be served cold, you can't make it too cold.

Besides the admonition to have plenty of ice on hand for a party, more than you think you'll need, our pros behind the bar offered a number of suggestions on how to handle ice, store it, use it in drinks, and frost glasses with it. Here are some of those suggestions:

- Ice can spoil. If you've had trays of ice in your freezer for months, chances are it not only has gone stale, it undoubtedly has picked up food odors. Ice should be made as close to the time of a party as possible. If that puts too much of a burden on your time and freezer capacity, buy bags of ice, checking first to see that the ice has been made with bottled or purified water. Tainted ice cubes will ruin a drink—even one made with the best of premium liquors.

- Ice trays can get dirty. Wash them before making ice. Ice can stick together. Ice should be cold and dry. Running water over an ice tray to help loosen the cubes will cause the cubes to stick together in the ice bucket.

- Ice can be broken, crushed, and made into mush. Many drinks call for cracked or crushed ice. This can be accomplished using an electric ice crusher or a blender. Failing these, wrap ice cubes in a towel and take a mallet to them. Remember: Cubes will dilute a drink less than crushed ice will.

- Ice can cloud a drink. Cocktails made with "clear" ingredients— Martinis, Manhattans, and Gimlets, for example—should always be *stirred*, no matter what Ian Fleming and his James Bond character claim. Using a shaker results in a drink with less crystal clarity. (More about this in the section on making Martinis.)

- Ice can be flavored or made to look pretty. Although this is not necessarily recommended, the authors have been treated to Martinis with ice whose water has been "doctored" with a small amount of vermouth. While this makes for a stronger drink because of less dilution, our pros behind the bar advise against it. A certain amount of dilution is preferable, they say. One of the authors has also been to a home party where the host froze tiny rose petals in each cube, resulting in a horticultural delight but a visually unappetizing Martini. Fancy, colored ice cubes may be fine for fancy, colorful summer drinks, but not for most cocktails.

- The average ice cube contains between 1 and 1½ ounces of water.

- To create a block of ice for use in punch bowls, remove the dividers from a metal ice tray before adding water and freezing. Or, fill up a thoroughly cleansed milk container with water, freeze it, and cut the carton away from the solid ice.

- Always put the ice in first before adding other ingredients to the mixing glass.

FROSTING AND CHILLING GLASSES

The ideal way to serve any cocktail is in a prechilled or frosted glass. Some of our professional bartenders go through elaborate rituals to achieve this; their techniques are presented when their approach applies to a specific drink recipe.

But if we accept that cocktails, particularly Martinis, Manhattans, and the like, should be served as cold as possible, it only makes sense to use a cold glass (just as frosted mugs or Pilsner glasses are the only way to serve beer).

There are many ways to prechill or frost glasses:

- Put them in a refrigerator for a half hour before use.

- Put them in a freezer before use. Fifteen minutes there will result in an even frost over their surfaces.

- Dip them in water and then put them in the freezer. A couple of hours and your glasses will have a frosty finish that will last through any drink.

- Before pouring a cocktail into the glass, fill it with cracked ice (a favorite method of our pros), stir the ice six or seven times, and discard it.

- Have a tub of cracked ice and insert the glasses into it, pulling them out one by one when it's time to pour a drink. This is the approach many professional bartenders use. The problem is it takes lots of ice, which presents no problem to top bars with ice machines.

Frosting is also a term used to denote the decorating of a glass's rim with such condiments as salt or sugar, even nutmeg or dried coconut for certain drinks. To coat the rim of a glass with salt or sugar, moisten the rim with a wedge of lemon or lime, then dip the glass into a plate containing a layer of coarse salt or fine sugar.

GARNISHES

"A cheery disposition is the best possible garnish," according to Joe Martin, bartender at Brandy Pete's in Boston. Besides a cheery disposition, there are as many possible garnishes as there are fruits and vegetables. The two most often used, of course, are lemons and limes. These can be cut in wedges but will most likely be made into "twists" to accompany drinks. Twists can be cut from any citrus fruit, including blood oranges, ugli fruit, kumquats, or even satsumas.

Many people think the addition of a twist of lemon or lime to a cocktail is purely decorative. Not true. Our participating bartenders all take pride in the way they prepare twists and other garnishes, and use them to provide just the right additional flavor to a drink.

We witnessed an interesting bartender demonstration one night, proving that twists are more than decorative. The bartender took a lemon twist, held it quite high over a burning candle, and slowly and carefully twisted it. The result? A "pop" as the volatile oil was ignited by the flame.

Citrus Twists

Cutting the perfect twist takes some practice, but once the technique has been mastered, you'll appear to your guests to have spent most of your adult life behind bars.

Using a lime as an example, cut off both ends with a sharp paring knife so that some of the fruit shows. Then, with that same knife, cut slits down the length of the fruit, keeping your cuts about a quarter inch from each other. Cut only through the colored surface of the peel, not deep enough to reach the white undersurface. The aromatic and flavorful oils are in the colored skin, not beneath. Carefully pull the ¼-inch-wide strips from the fruit, which gives you a dozen or so twists. Our bartenders prefer them to be about an inch long, so cut them into that length.

When a twist is called for in a drink recipe, or if you've decided to add one whether the recipe says to or not, twist the peel, with the colored side down, over the drink to release the oil and aroma. Then, rub the rim of the glass with the colored side and drop the twist into the drink.

Some of our participating bartenders use another technique for obtaining twists from lemons and limes. They begin by cutting off the top and bottom of the fruit, or the "knobs" as they're frequently called. Next, they make a single cut through the peel from top to bottom. Now, they insert the flat spoon portion of a bar spoon into the cut and maneuver it to separate the whole peel from the inside fruit. Once separated, they cut the peel into twists, and use the pulp for making fresh juice.

MUDDLING

Some popular drink recipes, most notably the Mint Julep, call for certain ingredients to be "muddled" before they are added to the drink. Muddling is the crushing of ingredients together so that their individual flavors are consistently and properly blended. If you're preparing for a large Kentucky Derby party at which Mint Juleps will be featured, you'll want to muddle in advance, preferably using a ceramic mortar and pestle. If you're muddling one drink at a time, and haven't purchased a muddling set, place the ingredients in the bottom of your mixing glass (be sure it's strong; you might want to hold it in a towel in the event it breaks in your hand) and use the back of your bar spoon as a pestle. Either way, muddling releases the lovely flavors of mint sprigs, sugar, herbs, bitters, or fruit when those condiments are called for in a recipe.

PARTING ADVICE

There are dozens of other tricks of the trade offered by our bartenders at the world's greatest bars, most of them concerning specific drink recipes, which is where you'll find them—in the next chapter.

As general advice, here are two inside secrets from two of our bartenders: Robert Schwartz, barman at The Club Bar of Beverly Hills's Peninsula Hotel, says he received this advice from another bartender: "If you truly don't know what it [a drink] is, make it red, and put rum in it." Similarly, another bartender passed along the following to Patrick Negron of Seattle's Ray's Boathouse: "If he came across a drink request he didn't know the recipe for, he'd make it as close as memory allowed, then add a splash of cranberry juice." (Obviously, this works only for tropical drinks.)

Michael Shannon, who for more than ten years has been pleasing the palates of his customers at New York's famed "21" Club, adds the final trick of the trade, one shared by the majority of his professional colleagues: "Make sure everyone is aware of how happy you are to have them as guests. Relax—and enjoy your party."

CHEERS

We thought the home bartender might enjoy a list of foreign phrases to offer up instead of the familiar "Cheers!" If nothing else, it will establish your credentials not only as a skilled bartender but as a world traveler, too.

Japanese	"Kampai!"
French	"À votre santé!"
Chinese	"Nien Nien ne!"
Welsh	"Iechyd da!"
Austrian-German	"Prösit!"
Greek	"Eis igian!"
Danish	"Skal!"
Russian	"Na zdrovia!"
Dutch	"Proost!"
Irish	"Slante!"
Israeli	"L'chaim!"
Spanish	"Salud!"
Zulu	"Oogy wawa!"
Italian	"A la salute!"

How to Make
the Most Popular Drinks:
From Martinis to Margaritas
to Daiquiris and More

The Martini

There is no longer a true "classic" Martini, except in the sense that for the purist, only gin and vermouth are to be used. All the variations—vodka, rum, tequila, and dozens of other substitutes—are, to those purists, a cruel hoax.

Because of the popularity of vodka among today's younger set, a bartender, home-style or professional, can no longer assume that when someone asks for "a Martini," they mean gin and vermouth. Chances are they don't, especially if they're younger than forty. These days, anyone ordering a Martini must be asked whether he or she wishes gin or vodka. Sixty years ago, ordering a Martini meant receiving a drink containing gin and vermouth in equal amounts. At the other extreme, Ernest Hemingway had his character in *Across the River and into the Trees* drink Montgomery Martinis, fifteen parts gin, one part vermouth. The noted author named the drink after Field Marshall Montgomery, who commanded the British Eighth Army in North

IN SEARCH OF THE REALLY DRY MARTINI

Justin Barbey, bartender at The China Club, Paris, makes an extra-dry Martini this way: Pour gin or vodka into a mixing glass with ice. When properly chilled, strain the mixture into a cocktail glass. *Spray* a cloud of Noilly Prat on top. (Any old atomizer will do. Just make sure it's clean.)

Overheard at The Anchor Bar in Buffalo: "I want a *really* dry Martini. Just put some vermouth in the air conditioning."

A friend, in the process of making himself a dry Martini, called his significant other and asked her to hold a vermouth bottle near the phone.

The search for the perfect dry Martini is never ending, and has spawned all sorts of approaches. Filmmaker Luis Buñuel, who allegedly took as much care mixing his Martinis as he did setting up a shot in one of his films, once said: "Connoisseurs . . . suggest simply allowing a ray of sunlight to shine through a bottle of Noilly Prat before it hits the bottle of gin."

Hammacher Schlemmer offered devices such as a calibrated vermouth dropper, to go with other gadgets designed to appeal to those searching for bone-dry Martinis.

This obsession created a backlash in certain circles. A 1952 article in *The New York Times Magazine* said, in part, "The affliction that is cutting down the productive time in the office and destroying the benign temper of most of the bartenders is the thing called the *very* dry Martini. It is a mass madness . . . which may very well earn for this decade the name of the Numb (or Glazed) Fifties."

The authors of *The World's Best Bartenders' Guide* were brought up short one night in a Manhattan bar. A member of their party, a sophisticated woman who enjoyed her Martinis very dry, tasted the drink served her, then waved for the bartender.

"I asked for a very dry Martini," she said sweetly. "This has too much vermouth."

The bartender replied, with a smile, "Lady, this bar hasn't seen a bottle of vermouth in twenty years."

> **Perhaps the glass had a soap residue, or the ice was tainted. No matter. For lovers of dry Martinis, they can never be dry enough, even when they are.**

Africa during World War II. Montgomery, it was alleged, refused to attack his German foe, Ernst Rommel, also known as "The Desert Fox," unless he had a fifteen-to-one advantage in manpower.

Our home bartenders might want to emulate the dramatic approach to making a Martini of Ray Bond, bartender at The Mansion on Turtle Creek bar in Dallas:

"I prefer to use a glass tumbler when chilling the liquor. It could be seen as a neurotic habit on my part, but there is an aspect of cleanliness about glass which I like.

"I pour the liquor over ice in the tumbler, then place the tumbler in a bed of ice. While the liquor is chilling, I do the same with the glass. I don't like to pull a glass from the stale air of a cooler. Odors commingle in a fridge, and odors affect flavors. I form a large mound of ice within and above the glass. I mold it with my hands until the ice melts together. With practice, a tall, spectacular mound of ice will hold itself in the glass. It makes for lots of 'oohs' and 'aahs' from bar patrons.

"Above the ice mound I drizzle a little vermouth. It doesn't take much, but without the vermouth you don't have a Martini. It's nothing more than a chilled glass of booze. Through capillary action, the vermouth trickles through the ice to line the glass ever so faintly, which is perfect.

"After a minute or two, the ice can be discarded from the glass. Into the chilled, lined glass you may now strain the liquor and add the garnish. I shake only if requested, not for fear of bruising it—that's silly. Shaking leaves small shards of ice, which will eventually melt and water down the Martini. I prefer to let the ice work on its own.

"It's a great way to make a Martini! A little flair and show go into the creation of a delicious drink. And that's what a good bartender does, incorporate style to make a tasty drink."

Martini Superstitions

The great comedian George Burns was known for his love of vodka Martinis. When well into his nineties he was asked whether he was slowing down, he replied, "When I blow smoke rings, I notice they're smaller and not as round as they used to be. And when I drink a Martini, instead of two olives I'm down to one."

Burns always stirred his Martinis exactly three times. Many of our professional bartenders have their stirring rituals, too. Patrick Negron, who holds forth at Ray's Boathouse in Seattle, told us the following: "One surefire way of making a perfect [not 'Perfect'] Martini was handed down to me by one of my guests, and I use it to this day. Always stir a Martini exactly seventeen times, then strain. A magic number? Who knows? But since I have used this technique I have never had a Martini sent back."

More than half of our bartenders from the world's greatest bars indicated they followed certain rituals of stirring, of handling glassware, ice, and utensils, etc. Interestingly enough, most of them claim that if they don't observe their drink-making habits, the chances of a drink being returned by a customer are dramatically increased. Home bartenders, take note.

Some bartenders have their rituals when shaking a drink, too. The tony life-style of fictitious characters Nick and Nora Charles (he was "The Thin Man" of book and television fame) was synonymous with Martinis. Here's Nick on shaking a drink: "See, in mixing, the important thing is the rhythm. Always have a rhythm in your shaking. Now a Manhattan, you shake to fox trot time; a Bronx to two-step time; but a Martini, you always shake to waltz time."

Obviously, there can be as many variations on the Martini as there are minds creating them. But let's never lose sight of the irrefutable fact that in classic terms, a Martini is a combination of gin and vermouth, garnished with either an olive or a lemon twist.

The introduction of vodka to this most sophisticated of cocktails made sense. It's lack of a definable taste opened the world of Martini drinking to a much larger audience. Gin and its staunch flavor takes more getting used to.

No matter what variety of Martini readers of this book choose to serve, the key, the authors feel, is to approach the task of making a Martini with a certain reverence for its colorful, erudite past.

Martinis were a staple at the famous luncheon roundtable at New York's Algonquin Hotel, where such literary lights as Dorothy Parker, George S. Kaufman, Robert Benchley, Harpo Marx, and P. G. Wodehouse gathered each day to share their keenly honed wit and occasional wisdom. It was Benchley who quipped after arriving for lunch soaked from a sudden rainstorm, "I must get out of these wet clothes and into a dry Martini."

But it was Dorothy Parker who penned the most famous ode to the Martini:

I love to drink Martinis,
Two at the very most
Three, I'm under the table
Four, I'm under the host.

CLASSIC MARTINI

SPLASH OF VERMOUTH
3 OZ. GIN
OLIVE FOR GARNISH
LEMON TWIST FOR GARNISH

Fill a mixing glass half full with ice. Add the vermouth, then the gin. Stir together and strain into a cocktail glass. Garnish with an olive or lemon twist.

Variations
At The Bar at Morton's in Manhattan, Sean McCarthy soaks olives in vermouth. He pours out most of the olive brine, then fills the jar of olives with the vermouth. Adding one or two of the soaked olives to the gin provides the perfect amount of vermouth.

Marie Maher, popular bartender at Windows on the World ("The Greatest Bar on Earth") has created the next two special Martinis for the makers of Beefeater Gin.

THE WINSTON MARTINI

The Winston Martini was created to complement the flavors often found in cigars—nuts, vanilla, and spices.

1 OZ. CAPTAIN MORGAN SPICED RUM

1 OZ. GIN

DASH OF FRANGELICO

DASH OF ROSE'S SWEETENED LIME JUICE

LEMON TWIST FOR GARNISH

Stir together all ingredients (except garnish) with ice in a mixing glass. Strain into a cocktail glass. Garnish with a lemon twist.

THE PASSIONE MARTINI

Ms. Maher created the orange-heart garnish, which is an orange slice hollowed at the center that floats in the drink. Customers are so intrigued by the garnish that they order the drink in order to have one. Order one at her bar and watch how it's done.

1 3/4 OZ. GIN

1/4 OZ. PUNT E MES

ORANGE HEART FOR GARNISH

Stir together gin and Punt e Mes with ice in a mixing glass. Strain into a cocktail glass. Garnish with an orange heart.

Note
Punt e Mes is a bitter herbal liqueur.

Two other Martinis created by Marie Maher are:

APRITINI

1 1/2 OZ. VODKA
1/2 OZ. APRICOT BRANDY
MARASCHINO CHERRY FOR GARNISH

Stir together vodka and brandy with ice in a mixing glass. Strain into a cocktail glass. Garnish with a maraschino cherry.

MATA HARI MARTINI

1 1/2 OZ. VODKA
1/2 OZ. CAPTAIN MORGAN SPICED RUM
DASH OF FRANGELICO
DASH OF ROSE'S SWEETENED LIME JUICE
LEMON TWIST FOR GARNISH

Stir together all ingredients (except garnish) with ice in a mixing glass. Strain into a cocktail glass. Garnish with a lemon twist.

Club Lucky Martini

At Club Lucky in Toronto, barkeep Liz Cape whips up her signature Club Lucky Martini.

1 3/4 OZ. STOLI OHRANJ VODKA

1/4 OZ. WHITE CRÈME DE CACAO

ORANGE TWIST OR 3 BLUEBERRIES ON A STICK FOR GARNISH

Stir together all ingredients (except garnish) with ice in a mixing glass. Strain into a cocktail glass. Garnish with an orange twist or blueberries.

Tootsie Roll Martini

2 1/2 OZ. VODKA

1/2 OZ. COINTREAU

ORANGE TWIST FOR GARNISH

Shake all ingredients (except garnish) vigorously in a cocktail shaker. Strain into a cocktail glass. Garnish with an orange twist.

Our professional bartenders have concocted myriad variations on the theme of Chocolate Martinis.

CHOCOLATE MARTINI

Paul Mallory, bartender and manager of Higgins Restaurant and Bar in Portland, Oregon, receives a number of requests for his Chocolate Martini.

2 OZ. VODKA
1 OZ. WHITE CRÈME DE CACAO

Stir together all ingredients with ice in a mixing glass. Strain into a cocktail glass.

DEATH BY CHOCOLATE

1 OZ. VODKA
1/2 OZ. DARK CRÈME DE CACAO
1/2 OZ. BAILEYS IRISH CREAM
1 SCOOP VANILLA ICE CREAM

Blend all ingredients in a blender for 30 seconds. Serve in an old-fashioned glass.

Chocolate Martini Variations

Godiva chocolate liqueur comes in handy when experimenting with Chocolate Martinis. Mix a splash of it with 2 oz. of premium vodka, and garnish with the fruit of your choice.

Add a dash of Triple Sec for a pleasant variation on the Chocolate Martini theme. Ray Bond, head barman at The Mansion Bar, offers this as his best-kept professional secret: "When in doubt, add Triple Sec!" To any drink!

Add such ingredients, in small amounts, as Kahlua, amaretto, Chambord, Baileys Irish cream, or ice cream.

Montreal's immensely popular 737 Restaurant, Club and Lounge, with its multiple bars watched over by Pierre Beaunoyer, offers up these Martinis, among many. All are stirred with ice in a mixing glass, strained into a chilled cocktail glass, and garnished with a lemon twist, unless otherwise noted.

MARTINI 007

2 OZ. VODKA
TOUCH OF VERMOUTH

MARTINI PERFECT

2 OZ. GIN
TOUCH OF VERMOUTH

MARTINI DELUXE

2 OZ. GIN OR VODKA
TOUCH OF SCOTCH

MARTINI AMERICAN

2 OZ. GIN OR VODKA
TOUCH OF JACK DANIEL'S

MARTINI KAMIKAZI

1 1/2 OZ. VODKA
1/2 OZ. COINTREAU
LIME PEEL FOR GARNISH

MARTINI EXOTICA

1 1/2 OZ. VODKA OR GIN

1/2 OZ. MELON LIQUOR

1/2 OZ. FRESH LIME JUICE

MARTINI MARILYN

1 1/2 OZ. VODKA

1/4 OZ. CRÈME DE CACAO

1/4 OZ. CHERRY BRANDY

MARTINI BLUE DOLPHIN

1 1/2 OZ. VODKA

1/4 OZ. PEACH SCHNAPPS

1/4 OZ. BLUE CURAÇAO

We don't know what President Bill Clinton has ordered at The Capital Hotel Bar at Little Rock's Capital Hotel (barman Khalil Moussa cites bartender-customer privilege), but we do know that Mr. Moussa serves up what he terms "Martini #1" and "Martini #2."

This barman insists that vermouth *not* be included, at least not in his Martinis #1 and #2. It should also be noted that the addition of olive brine results in a Martini often referred to as a "Dirty Martini." Former President Franklin Roosevelt (bless him for many things, including signing the bill that repealed Prohibition) enjoyed Dirty Martinis.

MARTINI #1

1 1/2 OZ. GIN
DASH OF OLIVE BRINE
3 OLIVES FOR GARNISH

Pour gin over crushed ice in a mixing glass. Add olive brine. Stir and strain into a chilled cocktail glass. Garnish with olives.

MARTINI #2

1 1/2 OZ. GIN
DASH OF ORANGE BITTERS
SQUEEZE OF LEMON JUICE
LEMON TWIST FOR GARNISH

Pour gin and bitters over crushed ice in a mixing glass. Add lemon juice. Stir and strain into a chilled cocktail glass. Garnish with a lemon twist.

DUTCH DIRTY MARTINI

The Dutch Dirty Martini is a favorite among the fifty-four varieties of Martinis served to customers of Atlanta's Martini Club. Use a cocktail glass for straight up; a rocks glass when you serve it over ice.

2 1/2 OZ. KETEL ONE VODKA

1/4 OZ. OLIVE BRINE

3 OLIVES FOR GARNISH

Pour vodka over crushed ice in a mixing glass. Add olive brine. Stir and strain into a chilled cocktail glass. Garnish with olives.

GARDEN MARTINI

Barman Kevin Bennett also serves a Martini for the health-conscious.

2 OZ. VODKA

1 TEASPOON OLIVE BRINE

PICKLED ASPARAGUS SPEAR

HOT AND SPICY GREEN BEAN

Pour vodka over crushed ice in a mixing glass. Add olive brine. Stir and strain into a chilled cocktail glass. Garnish with an asparagus spear and a green bean.

At Brandy Pete's in Boston, Joe Martin likes to make his "bone-dry Martinis" with a hint of Dewars Scotch instead of vermouth. This, of course, is the way to make a Silver Bullet, whose recipe appears elsewhere.

It's unwise to attempt to discuss the making of Martinis without dealing with the fabled "James Bond Martini," introduced by the creator of that heroic character, Ian Fleming.

Here's the way Bond described his Martini in *Casino Royale*: "A dry martini. One. In a deep champagne goblet . . . Three measures of Gordon's, one of vodka, half a measure of Kina Lillet. Shake it well until it's very cold, then add a large thin slice of lemon peel. Got it?"

JAMES BOND MARTINI (AKA THE VESPER)

3 OZ. GIN

1 OZ. VODKA

1/2 OZ. KINA LILLET BLANC

LEMON PEEL FOR GARNISH

Shake all ingredients (except garnish) in a cocktail shaker. Strain into a cocktail glass. Garnish with a lemon peel.

Note

To be authentic, the drink must be shaken, not stirred. In *Casino Royale,* the first in the James Bond series, the drink was named The Vesper, after the heroine, Vesper Lynd.

The iconoclastic Bond dismissed the notion that shaking a Martini "bruises" the gin. We're sure he's right, although if our home bartenders want to be Martini correct, they'll *stir* their Martinis, unless, of course, a guest asks for The Vesper. If that happens, you can be assured that your guest knows exactly how James Bond made his Martinis, and will be watching your every move.

Bond mused later in the book, "When I'm concentrating, I never have more than one drink before dinner. But I do like that one to be large and very strong and very cold and very well made."

There are those, however, who actually prefer a "sweet" Martini. This is made with sweet Italian vermouth rather than the dry variety. Some of our bartenders, when called upon to make a sweet Martini, add a dash of orange bitters and call it a "Homestead Martini." A drop of Pernod results in a drink of yesteryear known then as a "Jeyplak."

SAKE MARTINI

Three of our bartenders gave us the recipe for Martinis made with Japanese sake instead of vermouth.

2 OZ. SAKE

5 OZ. VODKA

UNPEELED CUCUMBER SLICE FOR GARNISH

Stir together all ingredients (except garnish) with ice in a mixing glass. Strain into a cocktail glass. Garnish with a cucumber slice.

HIGGINS RESTAURANT AND BAR, PORTLAND

There are other imaginative ways to make a Martini. One bloke chose to do it by adding white crème de cacao to vodka (house, we trust). Hey, at least it was more colorful than the fruit juice Michael Jordan ordered, or the iced tea and lemonade Arnold Palmer bellied up to.

When he's not being so thoroughly tested, Barman Paul Mallory likes to mash a Higgins Kamikaze: Muddle 4 lime wedges; add ½ oz. Triple Sec and 1½ oz. vodka; fill with ice and shake hard; strain and serve up in a large cocktail glass.

THE LIBRARY BAR, THE LANESBOROUGH HOTEL, LONDON

The list of celebrities Salvatore Calabrese has served is endless: "From a Dry Martini Cocktail for the Queen of England to an 1802 Cognac for Joe Scott" (the most memorable bar moment in the author's life).

THE LIBRARY LOUNGE, THE CARLTON HOTEL, WASHINGTON, DC

Louis XIII Cognac and Coke? Condolences to Barman Nathan Yu. Trust it wasn't the same night that President Bill Clinton was sipping a Harvey's Bristol Cream.

Many studious visitors to the Library enjoy Nathan's time-tested Thyme Martini: 3 oz. Belvedere vodka, chilled and shaken, served in a cocktail glass with twigs of fresh thyme.

THE PUMP ROOM, CHICAGO

Bob Sorenson's specialty Martini is a tad more tangy. It's called a Dirty Bombay Martini and is made with Bombay Gin, olive brine, and olives stuffed with blue cheese. Not nearly as curdling as the oddest drink he's ever been asked for: Scotch and grapefruit juice.

GIMLETS

Serving Gimlets is one way to make a "pointed" statement to guests. According to *Webster's International*, the word *gimlet*, when used as an adjective, means "piercing, penetrating, or having a driving quality." As a verb, it's "piercing or penetrating." These definitions derive from the noun *gimlet*, which is an auger—when it isn't a drink. Which is why there are those who are convinced the drink's name came from a small, threaded auger, or gimlet, supplied to British sailors in the late eighteenth century to tap into the casks containing their ration of lime juice. Or maybe it was named after Dr. T. O. Gimlette, a British naval surgeon, who hit upon adding lime juice to gin to dilute its potency for sailors drinking it for medicinal purposes.

No matter. It's a fine drink, as noted crime novelist Raymond Chandler knew when he had his crusty hero Philip Marlowe sip Gimlets at every L.A. bar he haunted. In a sense, Marlowe did for the Gimlet what James Bond did for the Martini. Marlowe started drinking Gimlets in Chandler's superb 1953 novel *The Long Goodbye*, after being introduced to them by another character, Terry Lennox. Lennox told Marlowe, "What they call a Gimlet is just some lime or lemon juice and gin. . . . A real Gimlet is half gin and half Rose's sweetened lime juice, and nothing else. It beats Martinis hollow."

The only debate in making Gimlets is whether to use freshly squeezed lime juice or Rose's sweetened lime juice, which is concentrated and considerably sweeter than the natural product. Those bartenders opting to cut and squeeze fresh limes will sometimes add a half teaspoon of sugar to sweeten the drink. The consensus, however, is that Rose's sweetened lime juice not only makes the best Gimlet but was the inspiration for it in the beginning.

Lauchlin Rose, a Scottish gentleman, is credited with inventing Rose's sweetened lime juice back in the 1860s. He marketed his new product to merchant companies as an antidote to scurvy. Sailors carried the product to ports around the globe, including America, where Mr. Rose's "medicine" was introduced at the turn of the century. But the drink itself, the Gimlet, was certainly a British concoction, probably first mixed somewhere in the Far East; Singapore and Hong Kong both claim to be the drink's birthplace.

As with most drinks, variations on the Gimlet began to make their way into the bartenders' stable of cocktails. To serve straight up, use a cocktail glass; otherwise, a rocks glass.

CLASSIC GIMLET

2 OZ. GIN
1/2 OZ. FRESH LIME JUICE
LIME WEDGE FOR GARNISH

Stir together gin and lime juice in a mixing glass half filled with ice. Strain into a cocktail glass. Garnish with a lime wedge.

RUM GIMLET

2 OZ. LIGHT RUM
1/2 OZ. ROSE'S SWEETENED LIME JUICE
LIME WEDGE FOR GARNISH

Stir together rum and lime juice in a mixing glass half filled with ice.
Strain into a cocktail glass. Garnish with a lime wedge.

TEQUILA GIMLET

2 OZ. TEQUILA
1/2 OZ. ROSE'S SWEETENED LIME JUICE
LIME WEDGE FOR GARNISH

Stir together tequila and lime juice in a mixing glass half filled with ice.
Strain into a cocktail glass. Garnish with a lime wedge.

VODKA GIMLET

2 OZ. VODKA
1/2 OZ. ROSE'S SWEETENED LIME JUICE
LIME WEDGE FOR GARNISH

Stir together vodka and lime juice in a mixing glass half filled with ice.
Strain into a cocktail glass. Garnish with a lime wedge.

ORIENTAL GIMLET

Years ago, bars in Hong Kong and Singapore offered up what they called the "Oriental Gimlet."

3 OZ. GIN
1 OZ. ROSE'S SWEETENED LIME JUICE

Stir together gin and lime juice in a mixing glass half filled with ice. Strain into a large cocktail glass until two-thirds full. Top off with ice water.

THE GIBSON

The majority of our professional bartenders serve their cocktail onions on a toothpick. Early recipes for Gibsons had their makers simply drop the onions into the bottom of the glass. If you have toothpicks (and you should), use them. If not, drop the onions into the glass and proclaim yourself a traditionalist.

As with most popular drinks, the Gibson's origin is speculative. But after reviewing dozens of sources, we're confident it was created at New York's famed Players Club and was named after none other than Charles Dana Gibson, the turn-of-the-century illustrator who created the popular Gibson Girls. Gibson enjoyed drinking at the bar but didn't want to become fuzzy headed. He and the bartender, Charlie Connolly, worked out a neat little system in which Gibson was served plain water but with a cocktail onion in it to subtly mark the drink as water rather than gin. Gibson's drinking buddies, unaware of the scheme, started ordering their real Martinis with onions, and a drink was born.

Certain wags claimed the drink, with two onions, was actually named after the Gibson Girls themselves, and their obvious up-front physical attributes.

A Gibson is nothing more than a Martini garnished with cocktail onions rather than lemon twists or olives. But don't think the difference is all cosmetic; onions give the drink a distinct, briny taste, especially if more than two are used.

CLASSIC GIBSON

SPLASH OF VERMOUTH

3 OZ. GIN OR VODKA

1 OR 2 COCKTAIL ONIONS FOR GARNISH

Fill a mixing glass half full with ice. Add the vermouth, then the gin or vodka. Stir and strain into a cocktail glass. Garnish with cocktail onion(s).

Gibson Variations

DIRTY GIBSON

There's a "dirty" version of the Gibson, just as there is for the Martini: Mix same as above, but add 1 teaspoon onion brine from the pickled onions.

THE MURPHY

Here's another variation on the Gibson for your Irish guests: Mix same as above, but garnish with a radish.

WINDOWS ON THE WORLD, NEW YORK

Someone once ordered a single-malt Scotch with grapefruit juice 107 floors up at "The Greatest Bar on Earth." Even less discriminating was comedian Alan King: "It's all garbage to me! Just make sure it's gin and the cheapest gin you've got. But don't spare the lime!"

THE MANHATTAN

Although the Manhattan is not nearly as popular as the Martini, it ranks alongside it as a drink of sophistication. Those who order it establish themselves as being above the madding crowd, secure in who they are, and possessed of a keenly honed palate. It certainly isn't a cocktail invented to give rich older women a sophisticated excuse to imbibe in the afternoon. It *is* a city cocktail, however, although the authors urge you to indulge yourself in some ironic juxtaposition by sipping a Manhattan in the country next time the leaves are changing color, the frost is on the pumpkin, and the aroma of barbecue has faded.

Historians of the spirits world point to the year 1874 as the birthdate of the Manhattan, first served at, and named after, the New York club of the same name. The drink purportedly was created in honor of Lady Randolph Churchill, Brooklyn-born mum of Sir Winston, who took the first sip at a party at the club. Of course, there are no remaining eyewitnesses.

While Sir Winston Churchill's mother may have become a cocktail legend with the invention of the Manhattan, Winnie himself was briefly a pub owner, proprietor of the seaside Londonderry Arms in Carnlough, Northern Ireland. Today, the Londonderry Arms is a very good hotel with excellent service and cuisine and, as you might expect, a classic pub.

What is for sure is that the Manhattan, like the Martini, has evolved from a drink once made with equal parts whiskey and vermouth, to one in which the vermouth plays a minor role. In the Manhattan's case, the evolution has included experimentation with dry rather than sweet vermouth to create a Dry Manhattan, and a mix of both dry and sweet vermouths to concoct a Perfect Manhattan.

There is a current school of thought, with which we agree, that Manhattans should be made with American whiskey. Our favorite is Old Grand-Dad bourbon. In a Dry Manhattan, the vermouth balances the heavy bourbon taste; in a Manhattan, it's sweet enough for us to understand why it's an afternoon favorite of octogenarians; in a Perfect Manhattan, it makes a near-perfect drink on a crisp, cool autumn evening.

Brian Finegold, the bar manager at Jardines Jazz Club in Kansas City, likes to pour the vermouth over the ice and then add the whiskey. "With the vermouth in first," Brian explains, "it's easy to adjust the whiskey to taste."

Gary Egan at Pete's Tavern in New York City makes his Manhattans with as much as one-third vermouth, explaining, "It blends nicely with the harsh-tasting whiskey."

Which sums up the choices Manhattan lovers have: a Manhattan, a Dry Manhattan, or a Perfect Manhattan.

CLASSIC MANHATTAN

2 OZ. WHISKEY
3/4 OZ. SWEET VERMOUTH
DASH OF BITTERS
MARASCHINO CHERRY FOR GARNISH

Stir whiskey, vermouth, and bitters in a mixing glass half filled with ice. Strain and pour into a cocktail glass. Garnish with a maraschino cherry.

THE CALABRESE MANHATTAN

Salvatore Calabrese, whose legend as a mixologist and historian grows with each drink passed across the bar at London's Lanesborough Hotel, makes his Manhattan this way:

1 3/4 OZ. CANADIAN CLUB WHISKEY
2/3 OZ. SWEET VERMOUTH
DASH OF ANGOSTURA BITTERS
MARASCHINO CHERRY FOR GARNISH

Stir whiskey, vermouth, and bitters in a mixing glass half filled with ice. Strain and pour into a cocktail glass. Garnish with a maraschino cherry.

DRY MANHATTAN

2 OZ. BLENDED WHISKEY
3/4 OZ. DRY VERMOUTH
DASH OF BITTERS
LEMON TWIST FOR GARNISH

Stir whiskey, vermouth, and bitters in a mixing glass half filled with ice. Strain and pour into a cocktail glass. Garnish with a lemon twist.

Note

While a maraschino cherry is the proper garnish for a Manhattan, a twist of lemon is more historically correct for a Dry Manhattan.

PERFECT MANHATTAN

The sweet vermouth blends nicely with the harsh-tasting whiskey.

2 1/2 OZ. BLENDED WHISKEY

1/2 OZ. SWEET VERMOUTH

1/2 OZ. DRY VERMOUTH

DASH OF BITTERS

LEMON TWIST OR MARASCHINO CHERRY FOR GARNISH

Stir whiskey, vermouths, and bitters in a mixing glass half filled with ice. Strain and pour into a cocktail glass. Garnish with a lemon twist or a maraschino cherry.

RAINBOW ROOM "CLASSIC MANHATTAN"

The "Classic Manhattan" is one of Dale DeGroff's signature cocktails at the legendary Rainbow Room in the heart of midtown Manhattan. You can sit next to floor-to-ceiling windows atop the skyscraper, scan the length and breadth of the throbbing megalopolis below, and sip this beauty:

2 OZ. BOURBON

1 OZ. ITALIAN SWEET VERMOUTH

2 DASHES OF ANGOSTURA BITTERS

MARASCHINO CHERRY FOR GARNISH

Stir bourbon, vermouth, and bitters in a mixing glass half filled with ice. Strain and pour into a cocktail glass. Garnish with a maraschino cherry.

Note

DeGroff uses 2 dashes of bitters to give the drink a taste different from that of Manhattans in which only a single dash is called for.

OUR PERFECT MANHATTAN

Here's our blend for the country in autumn.

1/2 OZ. SWEET VERMOUTH
1/2 OZ. DRY VERMOUTH
DASH OF ANGOSTURA BITTERS
3 OZ. OLD GRAND-DAD BOURBON, 86 PROOF

Pour the vermouths over ice in a mixing glass. Add the bitters and bourbon. Stir and strain into a chilled cocktail glass.

RUM MANHATTAN

2 OZ. RUM
1/2 OZ. SWEET VERMOUTH
1/2 OZ. DRY VERMOUTH
MARASCHINO CHERRY FOR GARNISH

Stir rum and vermouths in a mixing glass half filled with ice. Strain and pour into a cocktail glass. Garnish with a maraschino cherry.

RAINBOW ROOM, NEW YORK

A guy asked Barman Dale DeGroff to stuff his olives with anchovies before slipping them into a Martini. Sound slapstick enough?

Dale would have preferred to serve up a Ritz Cocktail: 2 parts cognac, 1 part Cointreau, 2 splashes maraschino liqueur, juice of ¼ lemon, and Champagne; stir all ingredients except the Champagne in a mixing glass; strain into a cocktail glass; fill with Champagne; garnish with a burnt orange peel.

Dale also serves a Classic Manhattan (page 112).

Rainbow's Orange Breeze: 1 oz. Stoli Ohranj vodka, 1 oz. Cointreau, 4 oz. orange juice, and 2 oz. cranberry juice; pour over ice in a goblet; garnish with a thin orange slice.

TEQUILA MANHATTAN

2 OZ. TEQUILA
1/2 OZ. SWEET VERMOUTH
MARASCHINO CHERRY FOR GARNISH

Stir tequila and vermouth in a mixing glass half filled with ice. Strain and pour into a cocktail glass. Garnish with a maraschino cherry.

ROB ROY

"Rob Roy" was the sobriquet of an infamous Scottish Jacobite and cattle thief. (One of the authors' Scottish ancestors was a notorious horse thief, but no drink was named after him as far as is known.) The drink named after Rob Roy is law-abiding, satisfying, and an important staple of every home bar.

Actually, a Rob Roy is a Manhattan made with Scotch rather than blended whiskey, and, like the Manhattan, there are three basic versions: Rob Roy, Dry Rob Roy, and Perfect Rob Roy.

CLASSIC ROB ROY

2 OZ. SCOTCH
1 1/2 OZ. SWEET VERMOUTH
MARASCHINO CHERRY FOR GARNISH

Combine Scotch and vermouth in a mixing glass half filled with ice. Stir and strain into a cocktail glass. Garnish with a maraschino cherry.

Variation
A dash of Angostura or orange bitters is added by some bartenders. Try it.

DRY ROB ROY

2 OZ. SCOTCH
1 1/2 OZ. DRY VERMOUTH

Combine Scotch and vermouth in a mixing glass half filled with ice. Stir and strain into a cocktail glass.

PERFECT ROB ROY

2 OZ. SCOTCH

3/4 OZ. DRY VERMOUTH

3/4 OZ. SWEET VERMOUTH

Combine Scotch and vermouths in a mixing glass half filled with ice. Stir and strain into a cocktail glass.

BLOODY MARY

In the 1960s the Bloody Mary did for vodka what Joe Namath did for the American Football League: legitimized it, spiced it up, brought it mainstream, and made it a champion. Though invented in the 1920s at Harry's New York Bar in Paris, the Bloody Mary didn't soar like a Namath pass until the late fifties and early sixties, about the time Joe was sitting poolside guaranteeing a Superbowl victory over the highly favored Baltimore Colts.

Our resident historian, Salvatore Calabrese, head barman at The Library Bar of London's posh Lanesborough Hotel, pinpoints the year of the birth of the Bloody Mary as 1921, the barman as Fernand "Pete" Petiot. After Prohibition ended in 1933, Petiot moved to New York to become head barman at the St. Regis Hotel (which still mixes a marvelous Bloody Mary). Pete brought his recipe with him and called it a Red Snapper.

Marketing mavens of this day might attribute the somnambulant reception the Red Snapper received to its name at the time: The idea of drinking a fish is not especially appealing. Recognizing a dead fish when he smelled one, Pete reinstated the drink's original name: Bloody Mary. *Voilà!*

There is more than one theory about how the drink ended up being called a Bloody Mary. Was it named after Mary I of England, who picked up the unflattering nickname "Bloody Mary" because of all the people she had put to death? Or was it a tribute to James Michener's wonderful character in *Tales of the South Pacific*, Bloody Mary, so named because her teeth were permanently stained red from chewing on betel nuts? Your choice. What is known for certain is that in addition to being one of the world's most popular drinks, the Bloody Mary is an excellent drink for home bartenders to experiment with to come up with their own individual spin on the basic recipe.

One of our bars, The Pump Room in Chicago, is where the concept of garnishing the Bloody Mary with a celery stick was born. As the story goes, a resourceful guest at the bar was served a Bloody Mary without a swizzle stick. Reconnoitering the immediate area for a solution, she spotted a glassful of celery stalks. American ingenuity took it from there. There are those who say it is bad form to garnish a Bloody Mary with a celery stalk; there are those who say it is even worse form to eat the celery. And then there are those of us who were brought up to believe it is sinful to waste food.

Sean McCarthy at Morton's in midtown Manhattan was brought up to believe that "Horseradish will clear the nostrils and give a good zing to any Bloody Mary." We've talked with bartenders who believe it is the quality and quantity of horseradish that makes or breaks a modern-day Bloody Mary.

Gary Egan at New York's Pete's Tavern won't take no for an answer. "Always use horseradish," he maintains, "whether the customer wants it or not (they'll like it). Use celery salt, salt, pepper, crushed red pepper, Tabasco sauce, Worcestershire sauce, two limes and shake. My secret? I add a little mustard."

WARNING: While the authors agree that horseradish is the key to making a truly *great* Bloody Mary, there are some individuals who are allergic to it. They're few and far between, and it can be assumed they know of their allergy and will avoid, or at least inquire about, drinks that might contain horseradish. But keep it in mind.

Vicki Roush at The Green Parrot in Key West finds that Absolut Citron is a "very refreshing" vodka to use in Bloody Marys.

"The Bloody Mary is a drink that was destined to be reinvented," says Robert Brady, barman at The Capital Grille in Chicago. "Try it with bitters, A-1 steak sauce, or even pureed roasted garlic!"

Rob Ashfield at the wonderfully boutiquey Hotel du Vin & Bistro in Winchester, England, likes to squeeze half a lemon into the mix rather than the usual ½ or 1 teaspoon. And he shakes them with energy.

Anybody who has watched the hit television program *Cheers* knows that the bar (Bull 'n' Finch in real life) claims the best Bloody Mary in Boston. In fact, it's the house drink and has been served without alteration for twenty-seven years. Senior barman Eddie Doyle "slipped" in revealing that one of the pub's secret ingredients in its award-winning Bloody Mary mix is a touch of clam juice. His special mix is now bottled and sold at Boston's fancy-food stores.

For a really adventuresome approach to the Bloody Mary, heed Ray Bond of Dallas's renowned Mansion Bar at The Mansion on Turtle Creek. Although Mr. Bond was reluctant to share his precise recipe, suffice it to say that his Bloody Marys contain fresh vegetables and herbs that have been chopped, diced, then blended with the establishment's famous tortilla soup, fresh from the kitchen. It results in a chunky Bloody Mary garnished with a carrot stick. The only thing it lacks is the American Medical Association's seal of approval, which might be forthcoming.

The Rainbow Room's Dale DeGroff instituted a wonderful Sunday Bloody Mary buffet, which any home bartender can copy. Put out a pitcher of plain tomato juice and a bottle of vodka (preferably encased in a block of ice), and place between them every conceivable ingredient known to have been included in Bloody Marys. Let your guests "build" their own.

But a word of caution is in order: Unless your guests *know* what's supposed to go into a Bloody Mary, you'd best be on hand to guide their selections, especially the amount of each ingredient they put in their drinks.

A Bourbon Bloody Mary?

The authors have a friend who always orders his Bloody Marys with bourbon. Maybe he was the chap who once ordered one at The Compass Rose Bar in the Westin St. Francis Hotel, San Francisco. Bartender Danny Woo, who has heard his share of unusual drink requests in the fourteen-plus years he's been serving customers at that most genteel of bars, remembers the request well.

Virgin Mary

A Virgin Mary, as we all know, is a Bloody Mary without the vodka. At least that's what we call it here in the United States. The British, however, call it a Bloody Shame, having changed the name years ago because of complaints from some waiters and waitresses who were devout Catholics and resented having to place orders for Virgin Marys. Leave it to the British to come up with a practical, sensible solution to a problem.

Salt on the Rim or Not

Few of our bartenders salt the rim of glasses containing Bloody Marys, although some do, including Frank McLoughlin, who mans the bar with aplomb at the Fado Irish Pub in Atlanta.

CLASSIC BLOODY MARY

2 OZ. VODKA

4 OZ. TOMATO JUICE

JUICE FROM HALF A LEMON, WELL SQUEEZED

1/2 TEASPOON PREPARED HORSERADISH

DASH OF WORCESTERSHIRE SAUCE

DASH OF TABASCO SAUCE

1 TOUCH EACH OF SALT, PEPPER, AND CELERY SALT

CELERY STALK AND LIME WEDGE FOR GARNISH

Combine all ingredients (except garnish) in a mixing glass with ice. Shake vigorously. Strain over ice cubes in a highball glass. Garnish with a celery stalk and a lime wedge.

JOHNNY CHUNG'S BLOODY MARY

Johnny Chung at The Bar in the luxurious Peninsula Hotel, Hong Kong, prides himself on his horseradish-inclusive Bloody Mary. This, of course, is a Bloody Mary made from scratch, as all our professional bartenders prefer to make them. There are on the market respectable bottled or canned Bloody Mary mixes that can be improved by selectively adding your own extra ingredients to them.

1 1/2 OZ. VODKA

4 OZ. TOMATO JUICE

2 DASHES FRESH LEMON JUICE

2 DASHES WORCESTERSHIRE SAUCE

2 DASHES CELERY SALT

BLACK PEPPER TO TASTE

2 BAR SPOONS PREPARED HORSERADISH

CELERY STALK AND LIME WEDGE FOR GARNISH

Combine all ingredients (except garnish) in a mixing glass with ice. Shake vigorously. Strain over ice cubes in a highball glass. Garnish with a celery stalk and a lime wedge.

ROBERTO'S BLOODY MARY

Roberto Tondo of The Whisky Bar at the Athenaeum Hotel, London, makes a spicy Bloody Mary using Absolut Peppar vodka.

1 3/4 OZ. PEPPAR ABSOLUT VODKA

2 DASHES WORCESTERSHIRE SAUCE

2 DASHES FRESH LEMON JUICE

1/2 TSP. DIJON MUSTARD

TOMATO JUICE

PINCH OF SALT

Combine vodka, Worcestershire sauce, lemon juice, mustard, tomato juice, and salt in a mixing glass with ice. Shake vigorously. Strain over lots of ice cubes in a highball glass.

J BAR BLOODY MARY MIX

With a colorful name like Grayson Stover, she should have been in movies. As bar manager of the historic J Bar in the Hotel Jerome, Aspen, Colorado, Grayson serves up a great Bloody Mary to many a celebrity, and it keeps them coming back. She leaves the ratio of measurements up to you (use the classic recipe as your guide).

V-8 VEGETABLE JUICE
GREY POUPON DIJON MUSTARD
CELERY SALT
PEPPER
PREPARED HORSERADISH
DILL WEED
SWEET-AND-SOUR MIX
LEMON AND LIME JUICE
WORCESTERSHIRE SAUCE

Combine all ingredients in a mixing glass with ice. Shake vigorously. Strain into a highball glass.

DON MILLS'S BLOODY MARY

Head bartender Don Mills at The Bar at the Hotel Bel-Air, Los Angeles, has been asked for his Bloody Mary mix recipe so often, he's had it printed out. He leaves the ratio of measurements up to you (use the classic recipe as your guide).

Achieving just the right balance of these ingredients will take experimentation (not an unpleasant task). Of course, you can always stop by the Bel-Air and take notes while Don performs his magic behind the bar.

HORSERADISH SAUCE

SWEET-AND-SOUR MIX

LEA & PERRINS WORCESTERSHIRE SAUCE

SALT

LIME JUICE

CELERY SALT

PEPPER

TABASCO SAUCE

BEEF BROTH

TOMATO JUICE

VODKA

CELERY STALK AND LIME WEDGE FOR GARNISH

Combine all ingredients (except garnish) in a mixing glass with ice. Shake vigorously. Strain into a highball glass. Garnish with a celery stalk and a lime wedge.

Variation
Some bartenders refer to any Bloody Mary with beef broth as a Bloody Bull, a tip of the hat to the Bullshot.

MICHAEL SHANNON'S DANISH MARY

Michael Shannon, barman of note at New York's "21" Club, developed his own version of a Bloody Mary using aquavit rather than vodka. He calls it a Danish Mary.

1 1/2 OZ. AQUAVIT

1/4 OZ. FRESH LEMON JUICE

4 OZ. TOMATO JUICE

1/4 OZ. WORCESTERSHIRE SAUCE

SALT AND FRESHLY GROUND PEPPER

DASH OF TABASCO SAUCE

ROASTED CARAWAY SEEDS FOR GARNISH

Combine all ingredients (except garnish) in a mixing glass with ice. Shake vigorously. Strain into a highball glass. Top with roasted caraway seeds.

BLOODY MARIA

Using tequila in Bloody Marys instead of vodka results in what's commonly called a "Tequila Maria" or "Bloody Maria." Manuel "Mannix" Ramírez, at the wonderful Casa de Sierra Nevada in San Miguel de Allende, Mexico, calls his tequila version a "Bloody Lupe." Once, a guest who was obviously suffering a terminal hangover and in search of relief asked Mannix to make him a Bloody Lupe and to mix it with a beer. He did, of course, with a smile—and psychic pain.

Use classic recipe but substitute tequila for vodka.

CASA DE SIERRA NEVADA, SAN MIGUEL DE ALLENDE, MEXICO

"Customers ask me to make Margaritas with Grand Marnier, or Piña Coladas with vodka instead of rum, or a Bloody Mary with tequila [a Bloody Lupe]," says Manuel Ramírez.

BLOODY HAMPTON

There are those who call anything made with Clamato juice and vodka a Bloody Caesar. We have a favorite recipe of our own that's made with Clamato juice; it's called the Bloody Hampton. If you're adventurous, float a clam in it.

2 OZ. VODKA

2 OZ. CLAMATO JUICE

2 OZ. V-8 VEGETABLE JUICE

1 TEASPOON WORCESTERSHIRE SAUCE

2 DASHES TABASCO SAUCE

1 SHAKE EACH OF SALT AND PEPPER

Combine all ingredients (except optional clam garnish) in a mixing glass with ice. Shake very vigorously. Strain into a highball glass.

BULL 'N' FINCH PUB, BOSTON

When Norm visits the pub after which *Cheers* was modeled, guess what he drinks? Beer in a mug. Sam Malone? Virgin Mary.

MINT JULEP

If the number of arguments over the proper way to make a drink indicates popularity, the Mint Julep wins hands down as the world's favorite. And that's remarkable for two reasons: One, the Mint Julep is a simple drink consisting of only three ingredients—bourbon, sugar, and mint. And two, most people, including Southerners, *especially* Southerners, have never tasted one.

At least that was the result of a survey conducted in 1992 by the Institute for Research in Social Science at the University of North Carolina, in conjunction with the Center for the Study of the American South. Seventy percent of those not from the South said they'd never tasted a Mint Julep. More revealing was the response of true Southerners: Seventy-three percent of them admitted the same. Add to this the fact that if anyone is likely to order a Mint Julep, it will only be during a single week in May when the Kentucky Derby is run in Louisville, Kentucky.

Why all the fuss? The debate erupts over such things as whether to leave the muddled mint sprigs in the finished drink; whether to add a little bourbon when muddling; whether to coat the inside of the glass with the muddled mixture; whether to use sugar syrup rather than undissolved sugar; whether to coat the rim of the cup or glass with sugar; whether the use of a straw is tacky; and whether a Mint Julep served in anything but a silver julep cup is, in fact, worthy of the name.

Much ado about nothing? Making mountains out of mixologists' molehills? Not really.

One of the pleasant things about classic cocktails is the tradition of making them. In writing *The World's Best Bartenders' Guide*, we wanted to instill in the reader a sense of pride in making drinks the right way, using a traditional approach. It's the authors' philosophy that as long as the home bartender is going to serve guests drinks, he or she might just as well do it like a pro.

It should be mentioned that the Mint Julep is synonymous with bourbon. There have been those who've created their own versions of this fabled drink using brandy rather than bourbon. They combine an ounce of regular brandy and an ounce of peach-flavored brandy with the sugar, water, and mint sprigs. We mentioned this to one of our bartenders, who said it's called a "Georgia Mint Julep." We take his word for it.

The word *julep* has been around a lot longer than Kentucky bourbon. Centuries ago, doctors termed anything that masked the unpleasant taste of medicine to be "a julep." Maybe its use in the drink called Mint Julep was intended to mitigate the harsh taste of early bourbon.

Who Originally Came Up with the Mint Julep?

The folks who put on the Kentucky Derby started serving the drink in the late 1800s. But there are references to it as early as the beginning of that century. Although bourbon is the main ingredient, and bourbon isn't bourbon unless it comes from Kentucky, there is strong evidence that the earliest Mint Juleps were whipped up in Virginia. After all, Virginia originally owned Bourbon County (Kentucky), birthplace of bourbon.

Other states occasionally claim birthrights to the Mint Julep, including Pennsylvania, Mississippi, Maryland, and Georgia. Even England and Canada have questioned whether this genteel American classic cocktail might have been created within their borders. To our knowledge, the Russians have yet to make such a claim.

Mint Julep Themes

Gary Egan, who manned bars in London, Paris, and Munich before gracing New York's quintessential stand-alone bar, Pete's Tavern, suggests using the standard recipe but sprucing up the presentation by having fresh mint in their original flower pots on the bar. That's what he does at Derby time at Pete's.

Dale DeGroff, widely acknowledged to be one of the country's leading experts on all things having to do with bars, spirits, and cocktails, always makes sure there are bowls of fresh mint on the bars at The Rainbow Room's multiple drinking venues during Derby Week. And he's created his own version of the Mint Julep, adding a touch of Apry, an apricot liqueur, to the classic recipe. He adds one ounce of it to the mint sprigs before muddling.

Some professional bartenders insist upon using only mint sprigs with red stems, claiming they have a stronger, aromatic flavor. Others add a splash of rum to the drink. Still others garnish with a cherry instead of a mint sprig.

CLASSIC MINT JULEP

4 FRESH MINT SPRIGS

2 TEASPOONS WATER

1 TEASPOON CONFECTIONERS' SUGAR

3 OZ. BOURBON

Place 2 of the mint sprigs in a silver julep cup, collins glass, or highball glass. Add the water and sugar. Gently muddle. Fill glass with crushed ice. Pour the bourbon over the ice. Garnish with the 2 remaining mint sprigs. Serve with short straws.

ROBERTO'S MINT JULEP

Roberto Tondo, the perfect host and bartender for The Whisky Bar at London's Athenaeum Hotel, makes his Mint Juleps this way (we've invaded England in more ways than McDonald's and Pizza Hut).

1 BUNCH FRESH MINT

1 BOTTLE BOURBON

SODA WATER

MINT SPRIGS FOR GARNISH

Put lots of fresh mint in a jug. Add a bottle of bourbon and allow to marinate for 2 days. Pour a shot of the marinated bourbon into a glass filled with crushed ice. Fill to top with soda water. Garnish with a fresh mint sprig.

Note

The absence of sugar in Roberto's recipe perhaps better mirrors British taste.

CHAMPAGNE MINT JULEP

The authors once attended a Kentucky Derby party in Manhattan where the host served Mint Juleps that included champagne.

6 FRESH MINT SPRIGS, PLUS 1 FOR GARNISH
1 TEASPOON WATER
1 TEASPOON CONFECTIONERS' SUGAR
2 1/2 OZ. BOURBON
4 1/2 OZ. CHAMPAGNE

Muddle 6 mint sprigs, water, and sugar in a mixing glass. Add the bourbon. Strain into a tall glass. Add ice cubes. Pour in the champagne. Garnish with a mint sprig.

MINT JULEP (PARTY SIZE)

Here's a recipe for making a batch of Mint Juleps ahead of time.

1 CUP CHOPPED MINT LEAVES
1 QUART BOURBON
8 MINT SPRIGS FOR GARNISH

Soak mint leaves in the bourbon for a few hours before the party and strain. Fill 8 collins glasses with crushed ice. Pour 4 ounces of the bourbon into each glass. Add more ice to fill glasses to the rim. Garnish with mint sprigs.

Note
There is no sugar in this recipe.

Mint Julep (Blender Style)

If you enjoy using your blender, try this approach.

3 MINT SPRIGS, PLUS 2 FOR GARNISH

DASH OF WATER

2 TEASPOONS CONFECTIONERS' SUGAR

2 OZ. BOURBON

Place 3 mint sprigs, water, and 1 teaspoon of the sugar in a blender. Blend thoroughly. Add 1 cup crushed ice and bourbon. Blend a few seconds more. Pour into frosted glasses filled with crushed ice. Garnish with mint sprigs. Sprinkle remaining confectioners' sugar on top. Serve with a straw.

The "21" Club, New York

George Burns needed a large martini glass for his double-vodka Martinis, even at the ripe old age of ninety-eight. Sean Connery, though, shattering the "007" myth, did not use a cocktail glass; he drank his whiskey-and-soda out of a tall highball glass. Ingrid Bergman sipped her vodka over ice, as did Elizabeth Taylor with her Jack Daniel's. And if you've ever wondered why President Nixon never looked happy, it might have been because he celebrated his visits to "21" with Perrier and Sweet & Low. Back when he was vice president, he drank white wine at The Bar at The Peninsula, Hong Kong. See what the pressures of office can do to a person?

The "21" Traditional South Side is a variation of the Mint Julep: Combine 2 oz. vodka (or gin), juice of 1 lemon, 2 teaspoons granulated sugar, and 1 tablespoon fresh mint leaves with ice in a shaker; shake vigorously to bruise mint leaves; strain into a chilled collins glass filled with ice.

THE MARGARITA

We've traveled throughout Mexico and thought the best Margarita we'd ever tasted was at the Acapulco Princess. But that was until we came across Mannix behind the bar at the Casa de Sierra Nevada in San Miguel de Allende. The test of a great Margarita is if it shivers equally both sides of the throat a moment after it slides down the middle. Mannix's Margaritas do exactly that, and then some. Of course, with more than fifty varieties of tequila at his disposal, he begins with a certain advantage.

Unfortunately, Mannix considers his Margarita recipe a "professional secret," and we were unable to cajole it out of him with sweet talk, intimidate it out of him with gringo boorishness, or pry it out of him with a muddler.

Fortunately, the Margarita is one of the most popular recipes with our other professional bartenders, and a particular favorite at The Green Parrot and The Blue Parrot bars, whose bartenders were eager to share their approach with us, and you—the home bartender. But first, a bit of history.

Legend has it that the Margarita was named for Marjorie King, a Hollywood actress who slipped south of the border in the thirties (as did half the population of the American Southwest during Prohibition) for an occasional cocktail. Marjorie was a guest at a ranch in Tijuana where the owner, Danny Herrera, named the drink after her.

But Ms. King isn't the only lovely lady claiming to have had a drink immortalized in her name and honor. There's a bevy of Margarets and Marjories out there who've made similar claims to fame. The authors toast them all.

Of all the classic cocktails, the Margarita has probably suffered the worst bastardization over the years, having been turned into frothy soda-pop concoctions by blender-crazed sun worshipers who think that as long as there's tequila in the mix and salt on the rim of the glass, they've made a great Margarita. And someone came up with the idea of freezing the Margarita—probably the same guy who dreamed up the concept of forcing a lime wedge down the long neck of a bottle of Corona beer. Odds are he wasn't an engineer with an educated palate. But because it would be presumptuous of us, even arrogant, to dismiss those who like their Margaritas frozen, we proffer a Frozen Margarita recipe in this section. Just don't let out where you read it.

Margarita Variations

Putting parrots first, in Audubon pro forma, reveals a Margarita/shady-people correlation. The Green Parrot in Key West bills itself as "A Sunny Place for Shady People." And The Blue Parrot in East Hampton, New York, was a source of inspiration for our pal James Brady, whose best-selling novel *Further Lane* lifted the lid off the Roland Eisenberg/Little Bit caper.

In addition to their moniker, these parrot people have two things in common: They look at life through a winking eye, and they love their Margaritas.

Vicki Roush of The Green Parrot likes to add "just a touch of orange juice to Margaritas. It brightens the color and sweetens them up, just a little. Gets high praises," she proudly proclaims.

The Blue Parrot's Margarita recipe also includes orange juice (there must be a parrot Internet).

Grayson Stover at the J Bar in Aspen also recommends the addition of orange juice, while Jim Martin at Boston's Brandy Pete's prefers fresh lemon juice.

Kevin Stewart of the Queen City Grill, Seattle, maintains that a Margarita is best with crushed ice.

Another champion of the orange, Tim Pieri of Harry's Restaurant and Bar, St. Louis, explains its effect in detail: "Adding a small splash of orange juice gives the drink a small but noticeable golden color. More important, it enhances the flavor of the Triple Sec. When used in conjunction with a great golden tequila (Cuervo, 1800, Sauza, Patron, etc.), the drink is as smooth and delicious as it can be."

Sean McCarthy of The Bar at Morton's didn't learn to make Margaritas growing up in Dublin, but he did when he worked at a Mexican restaurant in New York City. "The owner wouldn't let us make a Margarita unless we squeezed the limes in front of the customer," Sean said. "A Margarita has to be made with fresh lime juice."

Robert Brady at the Capital Grille, Chicago, maintains that the secret to a good Margarita is in the mixing. "A good 'Rita is at least three-to-one parts tequila over Cointreau. Use a good tequila, but not too expensive."

Ray Bond at the Mansion Bar in The Mansion on Turtle Creek agrees. So listen up, because Ray makes the best Margarita in Dallas. "I like to keep things simple, which is a bartending philosophy of mine," Ray says. "For tequila, I get no more exotic than Cuervo Gold. I really prefer silver tequila . . . it sends a gritty sting through the mix that will not be denied.

"I use straight Triple Sec and not Cointreau. I finish with a sweet-and-sour mix I make on the spot. A big splash of fresh lime juice and a heaping bar spoonful of powdered sugar. I shake the shake mix well to dissolve the sugar and create a frothy concoction. It's a shimmering beauty in a salt-rimmed glass, and the taste is the eighth wonder of the world." Now that's a cocktail made by a professional bartender!

CLASSIC MARGARITA

2 OZ. TEQUILA
JUICE OF HALF A FRESH LIME
1 OZ. COINTREAU
WEDGE OF LIME AND FINE SALT FOR GLASS RIM

Shake the tequila, lime juice, and Cointreau with ice in a cocktail shaker. Rim an old-fashioned glass with a wedge of lime and dip it into the salt. Strain tequila mixture into glass.

BLUE PARROT MARGARITA

3 OZ. SAUZA TEQUILA

1 OZ. TRIPLE SEC

1 OZ. ORANGE JUICE

3 OZ. FRESH LEMON JUICE

Shake the tequila, Triple Sec, and orange juice with ice in a cocktail shaker. Strain tequila mixture over crushed ice in a 16 oz. drinking jar.

THE GREEN PARROT, KEY WEST

When Lou Diamond Phillips dropped in, he had bartender Vicki Roush's full attention: "Watching that guy bent over the pool table was heaven!" she reports, while concocting the tastiest Margaritas this side of the Alamo.

How eclectic is The Green Parrot's bar scene? In recent memory, you could have sidled up to the bar next to George Stephanopoulous, John Goodman, Eric Clapton, or Charles Kurault (which we would have loved to do while there was still a chance). Whatever you do, though, behave yourself. Vicki's sidekick, Mark Devise, reports that the likes of David Carradine have been kicked out of The Green Parrot, and David Crosby of Crosby, Stills, Nash and Young, was booed out.

Mark's weird drink request is Monkey Piss, which he makes by pouring the "contents of the bar mat into a shot glass for that special drunk guy."

MALLORY'S MARGARITA

Paul Mallory of Higgins Restaurant and Bar in Portland, Oregon, takes a highly individualistic approach to making Margaritas, including the absence of salt around the rim.

3 LEMON QUARTERS

3 LIME QUARTERS

1 1/2 OZ. CUERVO GOLD TEQUILA

3/4 OZ. TRIPLE SEC

Muddle the lemons and limes in a cocktail shaker. Add the tequila and Triple Sec. Shake vigorously with ice. Serve in a cocktail glass with muddled fruit.

GRAND MARNIER MARGARITA

Pierre Beaunoyer, who sees to it that the hundreds of daily bar customers at Montreal's 737 Restaurant, Club and Lounge are satisfied, offers up this recipe for his signature Margarita.

3/4 OZ. TEQUILA

3/4 OZ. GRAND MARNIER

FRESH LIME JUICE

LIME WEDGE AND SALT FOR GLASS RIM

LIME WEDGE FOR GARNISH

Shake the tequila, Grand Marnier, and lime juice with ice in a cocktail shaker. Rim an old-fashioned glass with a wedge of lime and dip it into the salt. Strain tequila mixture into glass. Garnish with a lime wedge.

737 Restaurant, Club and Lounge, Montreal

Barman Pierre Beaunoyer has three varieties of "Caesars," all of which include: 3 oz. Clamato juice, a dash of Tabasco sauce, a dash of Worcestershire sauce, and a shake of pepper. For a Tequila Caesar, add 1¼ oz. tequila; for a Gin Caesar, 1¼ oz. gin; or for a Bloody Caesar, 1¼ oz. vodka.

Pierre prides himself on several other specialty cocktail recipes, including:

Cafe 737: Rim a cocktail glass with sugar; add espresso, ¾ oz. cognac, ¼ oz. Baileys Irish Cream, and ¼ oz. blackberry juice; top with Chicoutai and whipped cream.

Blueberry Tea: Rim a cocktail glass with sugar; add tea, ¾ oz. cognac, and ¼ oz. amaretto; top with whipped cream.

They all sound better than the Jack Daniel's, tequila, and Tabasco sauce some folks order; or Roncoco, Kahlua, and Southern Comfort on ice. Pierre serves plenty of Molson's, too: Montreal—Hockey Town.

Peach Margarita

1 ½ OZ. TEQUILA

¾ OZ. PEACH LIQUEUR

1 TEASPOON TRIPLE SEC OR COINTREAU

1 OZ. FRESH LIME JUICE

LIME WEDGE AND SALT FOR GLASS RIM

PEACH WEDGE FOR GARNISH

Shake the tequila, peach liqueur, Triple Sec or Cointreau, and lime juice in a cocktail shaker. Rim an old-fashioned glass with a wedge of lime and dip it into the salt. Strain tequila mixture over ice in glass. Garnish with a peach wedge.

Variation
Use any fruit; simply follow above directions, substituting one fruit liqueur for another, and garnish with a piece of that same fruit.

BLUE MARGARITA

2 OZ. TEQUILA
3/4 OZ. BLUE CURAÇAO
1 TEASPOON TRIPLE SEC OR COINTREAU
1 OZ. FRESH LIME JUICE
LIME WEDGE AND SALT FOR GLASS RIM
LIME WEDGE FOR GARNISH

Shake the tequila, curaçao, Triple Sec or Cointreau, and lime juice with ice in a cocktail shaker. Rim an old-fashioned glass with a wedge of lime and dip it into the salt. Strain tequila mixture over ice in glass. Garnish with a lime wedge.

Variation
For a Gold Margarita, use gold tequila instead of blue curaçao.

FROZEN MARGARITA

All right, we promised a recipe for a Frozen Margarita. Better yet, when you're serving Margaritas and a guest asks for the frozen version, confess

*that the blender is out for repairs, and offer a Margarita on the rocks.
Professional bartenders can't get away with this, but the home bartender
can. After all, in that castle called your home, the guest is always right,
except when it comes to Frozen Margaritas.*

2 OZ. TEQUILA

1 OZ. COINTREAU OR TRIPLE SEC

2 OZ. FRESH LIME JUICE

2 TEASPOONS SUGAR

LIME WEDGE AND SALT FOR GLASS RIM

LIME WEDGE FOR GARNISH

Combine tequila, Cointreau or Triple Sec, lime juice, and sugar in a
blender with crushed ice. Blend at high speed until frothy. Rim a collins
glass with a wedge of lime and dip it into the salt. Pour drink into glass.
Garnish with a lime wedge.

NEGRONI

The Negroni is essentially a Martini, but one that is given a distinctive
flavor by the addition of Campari, an apéritif with a decidedly bitter
taste. You either love the taste of Campari or find it hard to swallow,
even when mixed with gin and vermouth.

Like a Martini, a Negroni can be made dry or sweet. To serve
straight up, mix in a mixing glass before straining into your guests'
glasses.

Some bartenders, especially in summer, prefer to add a splash of
club soda to their Negronis.

Rob Ashfield, bartender at the cozy bar at Winchester's Hotel du
Vin & Bistro, treats his customers to Negronis made with a lemon half
and a lime half squeezed into the drink. Almost makes you want one
with your eggs in the morning.

The authors prefer their Negronis made with 3 ounces of gin and a half ounce each of Campari and sweet vermouth. What will your variation be?

Why "Negroni"?

You have two choices: Some say that Italy's Campari Company, makers of the apéritif, coined the name to distinguish this particular drink from many others using its product. Still, why "Negroni"? Others point to an Italian gadfly from Florence named Count Negroni who, it was said, flitted from bar to bar back in the twenties, ordering the drink enough times for it to be named after him. Whatever the drink's origins, the Negroni is a splendid concoction—*if* you enjoy the taste of Campari.

Note

Years ago a dry Negroni was also known by some bartenders as a "Cardinal II." Why? You had to ask.

CLASSIC NEGRONI (SWEET)

1 OZ. GIN

1 OZ. SWEET VERMOUTH

1 OZ. CAMPARI

LIME SLICE FOR GARNISH

Pour gin, vermouth, and Campari over ice in an old-fashioned glass. Stir gently. Garnish with a lime slice.

NEGRONI (DRY)

1 OZ. GIN

1 OZ. DRY VERMOUTH

1 OZ. CAMPARI

LIME SLICE FOR GARNISH

Pour gin, vermouth, and Campari over ice in an old-fashioned glass. Stir gently. Garnish with a lime slice.

HOTEL DU VIN & BISTRO, WINCHESTER, ENGLAND

Did Rob Ashfield use a cocktail glass when he had to make a Negroni with half a lemon and half an orange squeezed into it? Did he save the bottle from which Emma Thompson drank her Michelob? What would that be worth! And who would have thought that John Cleese is a simple Vodka and Tonic guy?

BELLINI

Some of our professional bartenders add a teaspoon of grenadine to the mix for color. One substitutes raspberry juice for grenadine.

Serving Bellinis to guests brands the home bartender as a sophisticated, worldly chap, literary and discerning, especially if the Bellini story is served up along with the drinks.

The drink was inspired by the fifteenth-century Italian painter Giovanni Bellini. Giuseppe Cipriani, founder of Venice's legendary watering hole, Harry's Bar, was evidently entranced by the painter's use of color, particularly pink, and envisioned a drink with that same hue. He took white peaches, which were plentiful in Italy in the summer months, pureed them, and mixed them with Italian champagne. The Bellini was born, and regular patrons of the bar approved. It's been the bar's signature drink ever since.

Although we did not include Harry's Bar in our list of the world's fifty greatest, it has created its own aura since opening in the early 1930s, due in large measure to the list of famous people who've regularly frequented it: Orson Welles, Ernest Hemingway (who drank his Montgomery Martinis there while working on *Across the River and into the Trees*), and Sinclair Lewis, to name a few; and because it is the birthplace of the Bellini.

It's a satisfying, gentle drink. Then again, isn't any drink made with champagne satisfying and gentle?

CLASSIC BELLINI

2 OZ. PEACH NECTAR
1/2 OZ. FRESH LEMON JUICE
CHILLED CHAMPAGNE

Pour peach nectar and lemon juice into a champagne flute. Add champagne to fill.

"21" CLUB BELLINI

Bartender Mike Shannon of New York's venerable "21" Club has taken the Bellini to new heights. Not surprising, considering his years of expertise behind the bar of a former speakeasy that defines upscale New York and that attracts demanding customers who know their drinks.

1 (8 OZ.) CAN CHOPPED PEACHES, DRAINED

1 GLASS OF WHITE WINE

2 OZ. PEACH SCHNAPPS

CHAMPAGNE

GRAND MARNIER

Place peaches in a bowl. Add the white wine and peach schnapps, and let sit overnight in the refrigerator. Pour peach mixture into a blender and puree. Fill stemmed glass with 1 ounce of the peach mixture. Add champagne and finish off with a couple of dashes of Grand Marnier.

Like going to heaven.

CHAMPAGNE COCKTAIL

The best use to which cognac can be put in a mixed drink is as a primary ingredient of the Champagne Cocktail.

1 SUGAR CUBE

ANGOSTURA BITTERS

1 OZ. COGNAC

3 OZ. CHAMPAGNE

MARASCHINO CHERRY FOR GARNISH

Drop sugar cube into the bottom of a champagne glass. Soak it with Angostura bitters. Add cognac and champagne. Garnish with a maraschino cherry.

BULLSHOT

Some of our bartenders add dashes of A-1 Sauce, Angostura bitters, salt (often celery salt), and pepper, especially coarsely ground pepper. The Bullshot is one of those drinks where individual taste reigns supreme. It's a salty drink; if your guests don't like salt, or their HMO has them on a low-salt diet, you might consider offering up something else.

In a sense, the Bullshot (sometimes broken into two words—Bull Shot—and yes, it's a variation on what the drink was originally called) is a Bloody Mary with the beef bouillon substituted for seasoned tomato juice.

Because our collaborating bartenders represent the cream of the crop, they're prepared to whip up Bullshots at a moment's notice, provided there's a stash of beef bouillon behind the bar, which there usually is. But in lesser establishments, devotees of the drink are advised to memorize the recipe or carry it with them, and to simply hope there's a can of Campbell's beef broth somewhere in the house.

Who came up with the Bullshot in the first place? There are those who claim that it originated back in the early fifties in The Caucus Club, a Detroit bar, undoubtedly in concert with a canned-soup salesman. If so, it's a classic example of what today's marketing gurus call "brand extension"—finding another use for a product already in distribution.

CLASSIC BULLSHOT

2 OZ. VODKA
4 OZ. CHILLED BEEF BOUILLON
DASH OF WORCESTERSHIRE SAUCE
DASH OF TABASCO SAUCE

Shake all ingredients vigorously in a cocktail shaker half filled with ice. Strain over ice cubes in a highball glass.

BENGAL TIGER

Our information, however, has the Bullshot created at New York's famed "21" Club, one of our fifty greatest. Michael Shannon, barman extraordinaire at this legendary bar, has moved on to a variation of the drink, which he calls the Bengal Tiger. Why? Why not?

It serves three.

JUICE OF ½ LEMON

2 (10 OZ.) CANS CONDENSED BEEF BOUILLON

1 ½ OZ. AQUAVIT

1 OZ. STOLICHNAYA VODKA

CRACKED BLACK PEPPER TO TASTE

DASH OF WORCESTERSHIRE SAUCE OR TO TASTE

DASH OF TABASCO SAUCE

ROASTED CARAWAY SEEDS AND FRESH MINT FOR GARNISH

Shake all ingredients (except garnishes) vigorously in a cocktail shaker half filled with ice. Garnish with caraway seeds and mint.

THE MOJITO

The Cubans are jovial, brilliant, outgoing, warm, and friendly people. One of the great tragedies of the rift between their leaders and ours is that we don't get to meet more of them. Another great tragedy is the relative obscurity in which has languished one of the great cocktails of all time: the Mojito. As a result, the Mojito rarely appears in cocktail books, and when it does, the recipe is usually off the mark.

Our insiders, Susan and Alan Schoenbach, recently brought back the original recipe from La Bodeguita del Medio in Havana, where the Mojito was invented, where Ernest Hemingway and Gabriel García Márquez wrote its praises, and where Brigitte Bardot sipped its sweetness.

THE AUTHENTIC CUBAN MOJITO

"The magical touch of this cocktail," explains La Bodeguita bartender Jorge Lorenzo Viqueira Lee, "lies in crushing the tiny branches of mint so as to extract the juice from the stem."

With the understanding that you'll have to substitute for the Silver Dry Havana Club rum (perhaps using Bacardi), mix this up in your home bar, sip it, share it, and decide if this is not one of the greatest cocktails you've ever tasted. While you do so, you might like to keep in mind Jorge's philosophy of mixology: "The essence of preparing cocktails lies in a creation of harmony, not in an addition or a diversity of flavors. An accurate dosage of the ingredients is necessary to achieve both the prescribed flavor and the strength in the desired mix."

This commitment to purity is the same that attracted Errol Flynn, Nat King Cole, Wilfredo Lam, Victor Manuel, Alicia Alonso, Lou Costello, Jimmy Durante, and legions of other luminaries to La Bodeguita del Medio for their Mojito.

It translates: "All that we're saying is give peace a chance."

1 TEASPOON SUGAR

1/4 OZ. FRESH LIME JUICE

2 TINY BRANCHES OF MINT

2 OZ. SPARKLING WATER

1 1/2 OZ. SILVER DRY HAVANA CLUB RUM

Stir all ingredients in a mixing glass. Pour over ice in a glass.

SIDECAR

The Sidecar is another cocktail whose origin is attributed to Harry's New York Bar in Paris, where it supposedly was named after a guest who arrived there in the sidecar of a motorcycle. Ahem.

Regardless of the alcoholic strength, one thing we know for sure about the Sidecar is that it must be measured carefully. If the Cointreau and the lemon juice are not equally proportioned, the drink will be ruined. Practice, get it perfect, and feel comfortable recommending a Sidecar to guests who are indecisive about what drink to request. It's a marvelous cocktail for which you will be remembered and admired.

CLASSIC SIDECAR

2 OZ. COGNAC
1 OZ. COINTREAU
1 OZ. FRESH LEMON JUICE

Shake all ingredients briskly in a cocktail shaker; pour into a cocktail glass.

LIBRARY BAR'S SIDECAR

Because the Sidecar's spirit base is cognac, we deferred to the worldwide dean of cognacs, Salvatore Calabrese of the Library Bar at the Lanesborough Hotel, London. Not surprisingly, his classic cocktail version of the Sidecar is a bit tamer than most American versions—a good recipe.

1 OZ. BRANDY (WHICH CAN BE COGNAC)

2/3 OZ. COINTREAU

2/3 OZ. FRESH LEMON JUICE

Shake all ingredients briskly in a cocktail shaker; pour into a cocktail glass.

HIGGINS'S SIDECAR

Here's a great Sidecar recipe from Paul Mallory of Higgins Restaurant and Bar, Portland, Oregon. "Fresh fruit is essential to this drink," says Paul. "A hard shake will help dissolve the granulated sugar."

Note that Paul uses Triple Sec rather than Cointreau. Many professional bartenders make this substitution. Your call.

2 LEMON WEDGES

3 LIME WEDGES

1/2 TEASPOON GRANULATED SUGAR, PLUS EXTRA FOR GLASS RIM

1 1/2 OZ. BRANDY

3/4 OZ. TRIPLE SEC

Muddle lemon wedges, 2 lime wedges, and sugar in a cocktail shaker. Add brandy and Triple Sec. Add ice to fill and shake vigorously. Rim a large cocktail glass with remaining lime wedge, and coat with sugar. Strain drink into glass.

Note

The Bar at Morton's Sean McCarthy also likes to include "a pinch of sugar" when making his Sidecars.

BMW Sidecar

For a mile-high Sidecar, we turn to Marie Maher at New York's Windows on the World. She's "upgraded" the classic recipe into what she calls the "BMW Sidecar."

2 OZ. BRANDY

1/2 OZ. GRAND MARNIER

1 OZ. FRESH LEMON JUICE

Shake all ingredients briskly with ice in a cocktail shaker. Strain into a cocktail glass.

Boston Sidecar

There's a version of the Sidecar invented in Boston and called, aptly, the Boston Sidecar.

1 OZ. LIGHT RUM

1/2 OZ. BRANDY

1/2 OZ. COINTREAU

1/2 OZ. FRESH LEMON JUICE

Shake all ingredients vigorously with ice in a cocktail shaker. Strain into a cocktail glass.

SILVER BULLET

The substitution of Scotch for vermouth in Martinis came into vogue in the years following World War II and flourished during the heyday of the "three-Martini lunch"—until, of course, President Jimmy Carter declared war on that civilized practice. It could be that young executives found it dashing, maybe even manly, to swagger up to the bar like an urban cowboy and order, "A Silver Bullet. Dry!"

The fact is, the addition of the unmistakable character of Scotch (top-shelf only) to gin in a Martini creates an interesting and pleasant taste.

CLASSIC SILVER BULLET

1/2 OZ. SCOTCH

2 OZ. GIN

LEMON TWIST FOR GARNISH

Pour the Scotch over ice in a mixing glass. Swirl to coat the ice. Pour out the Scotch. Add the gin. Strain into a cocktail glass. Garnish with a lemon twist.

Variations
Use any of the recipes in the Martini chapter, substituting Scotch for vermouth.

THE WHISKY BAR AT THE ATHENAEUM HOTEL AND APARTMENTS, LONDON

Back to the guy who ordered the Louis XIII Cognac with Coke from Nathan Yu (page 104). Did he catch a plane to London and only begin to develop a tad of taste before he dropped into the bar and ordered Louis XIII Cognac with ice and soda? Was he with the person who ordered a beer and blue curaçao?

Surely he wasn't with the Athenaeum's ebullient Sally Bulloch as she sipped her Champagne. Maybe he was with Luther Vandross when the singer drank a Coke with orange juice. Or, with Frank Sinatra as he ordered a Jack Daniel's and soda at a dinner at which fine wines were being served.

Barman Roberto Tondo would rather pour a fine single-malt Scotch, a very dry Martini, or any of a number of nameless specialties: Mix 2 parts Absolut Citron, 1 part cranberry juice, and a twist of lemon, and pour into a cocktail glass; shake 2 parts vodka, 1 part Amaretto di Saronno, and 1 part Tia Maria, and serve in a cocktail glass; mix 2 parts gin, 1 part Midori melon liqueur, 2 dashes of dry vermouth, and an orange twist, and serve in a cocktail glass.

LONG ISLAND ICED TEA

In our opinion, Long Island Iced Tea is a drink that should never have been invented. True, some creative, unnamed soul did manage to come up with a combination of ingredients that ends up tasting like nonalcoholic iced tea, but that's the problem. Young people latched on to it because it doesn't taste like liquor. It tastes like iced tea. It goes down fast and easy. "Time for another." And another. Until the effects of the tequila, vodka, gin, and light rum have done their predictable dirty work.

The authors know of more than one bar owner who has ordered bartenders to no longer make the drink, no matter how much customers demand it.

By all means, make Long Island Iced Tea for your guests and serve it proudly. But keep an eye on those drinking it. It sneaks up on you like a Stealth bomber.

Justin Barbey, head barman at Paris's China Club, recounts this story of a Long Island Iced Tea drinker at his bar: "I have seen more damage done with the Long Island Iced Tea than I have with any other cocktail. When the request came for a 'Long Island,' accompanied not by Coke but by Champagne, I realized we were dealing with either a raging optimist or a hardened pessimist. When the client eventually left, it was difficult to discern what kind of 'mist' he might be in, and it was more than likely that for the next few days he probably wouldn't know, or care."

LONG ISLAND ICED TEA

1 OZ. VODKA

1 OZ. GIN

1 OZ. TEQUILA

1 OZ. LIGHT RUM

1 OZ. FRESH LEMON JUICE

1 TEASPOON SUGAR

COKE OR PEPSI

Shake all ingredients (except the Coke or Pepsi) with ice in a cocktail shaker. Strain over ice cubes into a highball glass. Add Coke or Pepsi until the drink becomes the color of iced tea.

Note
Diet Coke or Diet Pepsi can be used for your weight-conscious guests.

The Anchor Bar, Buffalo

This is where you might have expected to find John Candy gulping a Long Island Iced Tea, which he did, or Jim Kelly sipping a Michelob Light (fans probably lined up to buy them), or Richard Simmons tippling a pink lemonade. Ivano Toscani, proprietor, says it's so. But then Ivano also says he improves on all the standard cocktail recipes by adding "just a sprinkle of magic salt." Maybe it's all that snow.

Black Velvet

If ever a drink was conceived to bring the huddled masses together, it's the Black Velvet. Think about it: Beer and champagne mixed together—Joe Six-Pack joining forces with the Park Avenue penthouse crowd—in one glass.

Of course, not just any old beer will do. It's got to be a dark porter or stout. Ideally, it will be Guinness Stout. Still, it's beer.

As for the champagne, no need to go top of the line. A decent, middle-of-the-road label will do just fine.

You have to admire anyone who would even think of pouring expensive champagne into a mug half filled with beer. Legend has it that the bartender at London's Brooks Club came up with the idea for the drink in the early 1860s, perhaps in recognition of Prince Albert's death.

One of the authors was first introduced to a Black Velvet while enjoying lunch with the late noted food critic and culinary guru James Beard. The two were dining at Eamonn Doran's Pub on Second Avenue in Manhattan, sipping pints of Guinness, when Eamonn broke out a bottle of Dom Perignon Champagne to celebrate the occasion. The corpulent maestro of the kitchen poured the champagne into the Guinness.

"What are you doing?" the author said, horrified at this spoiling of his stout.

"Making a Black Velvet," replied Beard, tasting, smacking his lips, and drinking again.

The author has been enjoying Black Velvets ever since.

Novelist and travel writer Tony Tedeschi, who enjoys trying different drinks, once asked a bartender in Miami for a Black Velvet. He watched as the barman poured champagne into a glass, then took a spoon, held it upside down, and floated some brandy over the champagne.

"I wanted a Black Velvet," Tony said.

"And that's what you got," the bartender replied.

Tony's experience is the only time we've ever heard of a Black Velvet being made this way, but it does sound interesting.

Tony was unimpressed.

Black Velvet

8 OZ. CHILLED STOUT OR DARK PORTER BEER

8 OZ. CHILLED CHAMPAGNE

Mix in a pint glass or beer mug.

Note

This is a drink that should *not* be stirred.

Half and Half

A Half and Half is a variation on the Black Velvet. It's a wonderful drink for the beginner who likes the taste of stout but finds it a bit too heavy. The

Half and Half is, invariably, a stepping stone from lager to stout, a step that should be made.

8 OZ. CHILLED STOUT

8 OZ. CHILLED LAGER

Mix in a pint glass or beer mug.

MANSION ON TURTLE CREEK, DALLAS

Ray Bond had a customer ask for a yolk to go with his stout. If Ray hadn't fulfilled the oddball request, he probably wouldn't have made our list as one of the greatest. But, of course, he did make the trek for the egg.

"With a stone face, he asks for an egg. 'Right,' I answer. 'You want an egg in your beer.' The customer insists, and is becoming impatient. I went in the back and retrieved the egg, placed it in front of him, and waited. He cracked it into his beer and chugged it down."

FADO IRISH PUB, ATLANTA

It's heartbreaking what some people will do to a good pint of Guinness. A customer once asked Frank McLoughlin, who prides himself on a perfect two-pour pint, to float stout atop fermented apple cider. Had Newt Gingrich or John Goodman been enjoying their pints at the time, surely they would have had a word with the miscreant. Oliver Reed likely would have remained concentrated tightly on his Glenfiddich on the rocks.

TOM AND JERRY

When we asked our bartenders about the Tom and Jerry, the most oft-heard response was, "Huh?" An American invention (created by Jerry Thomas, 1852, Planter's House Bar, St. Louis, later of New York City and considered the best bartender of his day), the Tom and Jerry is a splendid cold-weather, and labor-intensive, drink. Ironically, it garnered considerable popularity in England, where the winters, though rarely pleasant, are never as severe as those in the States.

Because mixing perfect Tom and Jerrys takes time, we suggest whipping up a batch of eggs, with the sugar added in proper ratio, in advance of your party. Combine all other ingredients in the proper proportion, depending upon how many drinks you intend to serve at one sitting.

Hot water can be substituted for the hot milk, although the authors prefer the version using milk. The egg whites and yolks can be mixed together in a blender, although beating them separately respects the tradition of the drink.

Why the name Tom and Jerry? The drink predates the introduction of the *Tom and Jerry* cartoon series. There were a couple of fictitious wags in London during the early 1800s named Corinthian Tom and Jerry Hawthorn. Was it named after them? Possibly. Perhaps the drink picked up its name from the British slang term for the antics of the fictitious duo, "Oh, he's out 'Tom-and-Jerrying.'" Translation: Living the high life; ladies beware.

We know one thing. Your significant other, client, or boss will be mightily impressed as they watch you tackle this chem-lab preparation of liquid rapture just for them.

Remember Tom, remember Jerry, remember yolk, remember white, remember all the rest to truly impress with a very special cocktail for very special occasions.

TOM AND JERRY

1 EGG, SEPARATED

2 OZ. LIGHT OR DARK RUM

1 OZ. BRANDY

4 OZ. HOT MILK

1 TEASPOON SUGAR

GRATED NUTMEG FOR GARNISH

Beat the egg white and yolk separately. Beat egg white until stiff. Add sugar; beat until white stands in peaks. Beat yolk until frothy. Fold the egg white into the yolk. Add the rum, brandy, and hot milk. Pour into a warmed mug. Garnish with nutmeg.

Note

Raw eggs may contain salmonella and should never be served to anyone who is ill or has a compromised immune system.

JARDINES, KANSAS CITY

Brian Finegold had a customer who ordered a Scotch, milk, and whole egg. "The guy said he didn't have breakfast," Brian says. "He [the customer] said it [the Scotch] kills the taste of the egg."

On the other hand, Lenny Dykstra, plug-chewing former Met and Philly, prefers Château d' Yquem when visiting Jardines.

MAI TAI

Trader Vic created this drink to welcome some friends from Tahiti to his Hinky Dink's bar outside San Francisco during World War II. He added rock candy, though the only reason we can figure for this was that the stuff was overlooked by the war-time rationing bureaucracy, and/or Vic couldn't figure out what else to do with the excess.

Our authority, Salvatore Calabrese, eschewed the use of the stuff in his recipe, which is as close to "classic" as you can get. Besides, where do you begin to look for rock candy?

2 OZ. LIGHT RUM

1 OZ. COINTREAU

1 TEASPOON ORGEAT (ALMOND) SYRUP

JUICE OF 1 LIME

2 DASHES GRENADINE

FRUIT FOR GARNISH

Shake all ingredients (except garnish) with ice in a cocktail shaker. Strain over ice into a highball glass. Garnish with fruit of your choice.

ZOMBIE

The Zombie, we've been told on site, was created at Parasteel, outside of Port-au-Prince, Haiti. At the time (1970s), Parasteel claimed to have the oldest, most authentic voodoo show open to the general public, and while we can't verify that this is where the Zombie originated, we can state empirically that we have seen our share of zombielike creatures depart Parasteel, having pounded a drum or two, danced a feverish step or two, rolled an eyeball or two, and, of course, sipped a Zombie or two.

A good Zombie is a drink to be sipped once a year, say on Halloween. Anything more, and you might start feeling like the walking dead.

Our resident cocktail historian, Salvatore Calabrese, writes that the Zombie was created by Don Beach, who owned the Don the Beachcomber restaurant in Hollywood in the thirties. We've heard and read this elsewhere. But if you're visiting Haiti, and a misty-eyed, tall, angular, and muscular Haitian man tells you in no uncertain terms, beneath a full Caribbean moon, that this is where the Zombie was created, you say, "Yes sir!"

The Zombie is a good blender drink. If you choose to prepare it that way, combine all ingredients in the blender except for the 150-proof rum. Blend at high speed. Strain into cocktail glass with ice. Float the rum on top.

2 OZ. LIGHT RUM

1 1/2 OZ. DARK RUM

1/2 OZ. 150-PROOF RUM

1 OZ. PINEAPPLE JUICE

1 OZ. ORANGE JUICE

1 OZ. FRESH LIME JUICE

Shake all ingredients with ice in a cocktail shaker (or blend as described above). Strain into a large cocktail glass.

THE BLUE PARROT BAR, EAST HAMPTON

Problems are one of Roland Eisenberg's specialties. "I was once asked if there are any drinks made with prune juice," he reports. His reply: "Yes, vodka and prune juice. It's called a Royal Flush."

Trust Roland didn't have this in mind when he penned his advice for the home bartender: "Never let your guests drink more than yourself!"

BRANDY ALEXANDER

Joseph Lanza, in his classic tome *The Cocktail*, describes the Brandy Alexander as being "among the most notorious of girl drinks. This concoction of brandy, Crème de cacao, and regular sweet cream was reportedly a favorite among Prohibition-era teenagers who wanted to ape their parents without relinquishing their passion for chocolate bars."

MARTINI CLUB, ATLANTA

Someone ordered Yoohoo chocolate drink and Remy Martin VSOP from "Marty" Martini.

Classic Brandy Alexander

2 OZ. BRANDY

1 OZ. CRÈME DE CACAO

1 OZ. HEAVY CREAM

NUTMEG FOR GARNISH

Shake all ingredients (except nutmeg) well in a cocktail shaker with ice. Strain into an old-fashioned glass. Sprinkle nutmeg over top.

Brandy Pete's, Boston

Joe Martin reported on his guests' odd-ball highballs: Hennessy, Baileys, and Kahlua; a bottle of beer with a milk chaser; and a Bloody Mary with a toothbrush.

Joe was once transported from the ridiculous to the sublime by "The Artist Formerly Known as Prince," when he ordered the soft drink formerly known as cola—Pepsi.

They should all just sit back and let Joe do the mixing. He'll whip up a California White Spider: Stoli Vanil, white crème de cacao, and a splash of Baileys, topped with milk. Smooth as if your momma made it.

Daiquiri

It would be difficult to prove that the reason John F. Kennedy wanted to wrest Cuba from Castro's clutches was because the Floridita Bar in Havana was the "Cradle of the Daiquiri." But the popular president did enjoy the drink when the sun went over the yardarm. Now, more than a few decades later, the privilege of visiting the Floridita is still enough of a reason to promote peace.

It was near the town of the same name that the Daiquiri itself was launched, not as a malarial treatment, as one rumor has it, but as a proper cocktail. American mining engineer Jennings Cox, on a long tour of duty in eastern Cuba, turned to the local ingredients to create one of the world's classic cocktails from Havana: light rum, fresh limes, and cane sugar.

The United States Navy facilitated the export of what was to become one of the most popular drinks on the planet in 1909, when Admiral Lucius Johnson brought the recipe home to Washington, DC.

While Kennedy, himself a naval officer, celebrated the link between Cuba and the United States that was forged by the Daiquiri, the relationship was formalized by the establishment of the Daiquiri Lounge at the Army and Navy Club in the Nation's Capital. Focal point of the lounge is a brass plaque dedicated to Jennings Cox.

At Pete's Tavern in New York City, Gary Egan says that a Daiquiri "must be really, really, really shaken. It should be frothy."

Don Mills at The Bar at the Hotel Bel-Air in Los Angeles drops a maraschino cherry into the blender when he makes a Frozen Daiquiri. "It gives color and a hint of taste," Don explains.

The authors have a number of friends who take their home bartending responsibilities seriously. They entertain frequently, especially in the summer, and have created their own signature Daiquiris.

One variation on the Classic Daiquiri, concocted by a magazine publisher, includes 2 ounces of coconut oil and a strip of coconut for garnish. We know he takes drink preparations seriously when you consider that in order to come up with slender strips of coconut, he must first bake the entire coconut to loosen the meat, and then carefully manipulate the flesh in order to cut the strips.

One summer evening, one of the authors was at the home of a travel writer who served her Daiquiris in a way attributed to an old-time bartender she'd once met. She filled a goblet with crushed ice, then gently pushed on one side of the ice with her thumb until the opposite side slid up the edge of the glass. She poured the mixed Daiquiris into the hollowed-out space. It was pretty, and unusual.

Bartender Joe Martin of Brandy Pete's is fond of substituting less-popular fruits in the Daiquiris he serves up at this venerable Boston bar. Kiwi and Mango Daiquiris are among his favorites.

Seattle's Ray's Boathouse, with a spacious outdoor cocktail area overlooking the fishing vessels, sailboats, and kayakers on Puget Sound, and with the soaring Olympic Mountains providing a breathtaking scrim, is known in the area for its Blueberry Daiquiris, made so cold that if consumed too quickly, the throat is anesthetized to the point that major surgery can be performed.

Made properly, the Daiquiri is a lovely, classic cocktail that every home bartender should become skilled at making.

CLASSIC DAIQUIRI

1 1/2 OZ. LIGHT RUM

1 OZ. FRESH LIME JUICE

1 TEASPOON SUGAR

Shake all ingredients well in a cocktail shaker with ice. Strain into a cocktail glass.

CLASSIC FROZEN DAIQUIRI

Try one of the variations below, but don't let your imagination stop there.

3 OZ. LIGHT RUM

1 1/2 OZ. FRESH LIME JUICE

1 TEASPOON SUGAR

Combine all ingredients with ice in a blender and blend until frothy. Pour into a cocktail glass.

Variations

BANANA DAIQUIRI
Add a banana before blending.

STRAWBERRY DAIQUIRI
Add ½ cup of strawberries before blending.

THE MEXICO

Jorge Lee at La Bodeguita del Medio, Havana (the Floridita's nemesis), has created a tasty variation of the Cuban standard, which he calls "The Mexico." Hemingway would order a double. "Salud, Papa!"

1 TEASPOON HONEY

¼ OZ. FRESH LIME JUICE

1 TEASPOON SUGAR

¼ OZ. SEVEN-YEAR-OLD HAVANA CLUB RUM OR SUBSTITUTE

1 OZ. SILVER DRY HAVANA CLUB RUM OR SUBSTITUTE

1 OZ. TEQUILA

Make a syrup of honey and lime juice. Blend syrup with sugar, rum, tequila, and ice. Strain into a cocktail glass.

The Daiquiri, Marie Maher

Windows on the World's Marie Maher makes her Daiquiris this way:

2 OZ. LIGHT RUM

1/2 OZ. SIMPLE SUGAR SYRUP

1/2 OZ. SPRITE

JUICE OF 1 LIME

1 EGG WHITE

LIME TWIST FOR GARNISH

Shake all ingredients (except garnish) vigorously in a cocktail shaker with ice. Strain into a cocktail glass. Garnish with a lime twist.

Moscow Mule

Some of our bartenders prefer to stir the vodka and lime juice together in a tall glass and then fill it to the top with ginger beer. This makes for a less potent drink, unless, of course, you increase the amount of vodka going into it.

Before our late pal Ansel (Ed) Talbert was aviation editor of *Travel Agent Magazine,* he wrote about the same subject for the New York *Herald Tribune.* During a visit to Moscow in the 1960s to cover aviation issues, Ed busied himself in his off-hours with a search for anyone who had ever heard of a Moscow Mule. He found none. As you might expect, the only thing the Russians thought went well with a glass of vodka was a quick flick of the wrist.

Surely, to this day, the vast majority of Russians have never heard of the Moscow Mule. It is, after all, the invention of a Los Angeles marketing maven named John Martin, who worked for Heublein & Company in the 1940s and was years ahead of his time in concocting a drink to help sell Heublein's Smirnoff vodka. The difference between Martin's efforts and those of many of today's promoters is that his resulted in a really good cocktail with staying power.

In those days, Smirnoff as a product was a Heublein dog. Martin had a lot of vodka to sell, and Jack Morgan, the owner of the Cock 'n' Bull in Los Angeles, was having a hard time selling a ginger beer he had concocted. They got together and found a copper company with a surfeit of mugs, onto which they stamped a picture of a kicking mule.

If our home bartenders really want to impress guests, find some copper mugs and serve the drink in them. Failing that, a highball glass will do.

The Moscow Mule—a stroke of marketing genius that resulted in a good cocktail.

MOSCOW MULE

2 OZ. VODKA

1 OZ. GINGER BEER

1 OZ. FRESH LIME JUICE

LIME WEDGE FOR GARNISH

Pour ingredients into an old-fashioned glass with ice and stir. Garnish with a lime wedge.

PRESBYTERIAN

It's always struck us that the drink called a "Presbyterian" represents one of those concoctions whose creator couldn't make up his or her mind whether to mix whiskey with club soda or with ginger ale. The answer was to use both.

2 OZ. WHISKEY

CLUB SODA

GINGER ALE

LEMON TWIST FOR GARNISH

Fill a highball glass with ice and add the whiskey. Top off with equal amounts of club soda and ginger ale. Garnish with a lemon twist.

TONGUE & GROOVE, ATLANTA

Michael Harris has "one for the books": "Picture if you will . . . you are a bartender at the most popular and socially diverse club in the city on your busiest weekend night. Madonna walks in with her crew of nine or ten and decides to order from you before adjourning to the privacy of the VIP area. Gosh, what an honor! As quickly as humanly possible, you accommodate her (ginger ale) and her friends while having to ignore the masses of deserving patrons. What, no tip? Even worse, not even a thank you? Surely, it is an oversight. It couldn't possibly happen twice . . . but it does."

Certainly, it wasn't anybody in the Madonna entourage who ordered the dry vermouth on the rocks, or the gin and Coke, or the cognac and Coke (check for fingerprints).

The Tongue & Groove is better known for its Woo Woo: 2 parts vodka and 1 to 2 parts peach schnapps mixed with cranberry juice and served over ice, straight up as a shot, or in a cocktail glass with an orange twist.

THE TOP OF THE MARK, SAN FRANCISCO

Is the name derived from the feeling you get after a couple of these? Must be the case here, where the specialty cocktail is the Earthquake: combine 1 oz. vodka, ½ oz. Amaretto, and ½ oz. Southern Comfort in a cocktail glass and stir.

No doubt a tremor of some magnitude could be stirred by any of the oddball highballs Barman Hank Cancel has been asked to mix: "I was once asked to fill a shot glass with just bitters," Hank reports. "Other unusual requests include a Bourbon Colada, a Martini with half vodka and half gin, a Campari and Dubonnet mix on the rocks, and a rum Cosmopolitan. The way I see it, as long as you are willing to pay for it and drink it, I don't mind making it."

SINGAPORE SLING

It's difficult to come up with a classic recipe for the Singapore Sling because the drink's origins are murky, and the "original" recipe is the subject of debate. The Singapore Sling is a derivative of what was known as the Gin Sling, a popular before-breakfast drink in the early 1920s.

It is generally believed that the Singapore Sling version of the Gin Sling was first introduced at Raffles Hotel in Singapore. That may be true, although there is evidence in the literature that it might well have been served up first in the port city of Sandakan, Borneo, and was called the Sandakan Sling. From there, it made its way around the globe to various ports of call, including Singapore.

Singapore Sling Variations

Few drinks have as many variations as the Singapore Sling; whiskey, Scotch, and brandy have been substituted for gin. But none of these should be called a Singapore Sling. They aren't deserving of the name.

One ingredient often added to the drink is an ounce of Benedictine. Many bartenders add a drop of brandy to the finished drink. Still others add a teaspoon of fine sugar.

Made simply, and according to the more basic recipe, the Singapore Sling is a fine cocktail, worthy of making for the most treasured visitors to your home bar.

GIN SLING

2 OZ. GIN

JUICE OF 1 LIME

1 TEASPOON GRENADINE

LEMON TWIST

CLUB SODA

Combine all ingredients except ice and soda in a highball glass. Add ice cubes and soda. Stir and serve.

ORIGINAL SINGAPORE SLING

Our London representative, Salvatore Calabrese of The Library Bar, maintains not only that the Singapore Sling was invented at Raffles but that its creator was barman Ngiam Tong Boon, who first concocted the drink in 1915.

2 OZ. GIN

JUICE OF 1/2 LIME

LIME PEEL

1 OZ. CHERRY CORDIAL

CLUB SODA

Combine all ingredients except ice and soda in a highball glass. Add ice cubes and soda. Stir and serve.

Note
The early versions of the drink were always stirred. But after modification at the hands of many different bartenders, shaking the ingredients became standard procedure and remains so to this day.

PINK LADY

You probably won't get many guest requests for a Pink Lady; our professional bartenders seldom do. But if you know that a guest you've invited happens to like them (or enjoys tossing down the gauntlet to home bartenders), make sure you have some heavy cream and a few eggs around.

CLASSIC PINK LADY

2 OZ. GIN

1 TEASPOON GRENADINE

1 TEASPOON CHERRY BRANDY

1/2 OZ. HEAVY CREAM

1 EGG WHITE

Combine all ingredients in a cocktail shaker half filled with ice. Shake vigorously. Strain into a cocktail glass.

Note

Raw eggs may contain salmonella and should never be served to anyone who is ill or has a compromised immune system.

HARRY'S RESTAURANT AND BAR, ST. LOUIS

One of the unusual drinks ordered here: equal amounts of Baileys, Frangelico, Jägermeister, and Scotch. It's called a Lithuanian Buttplug. Probably concocted by Count von Beavis.

Beachheaded in Bud country, barman Richard Ross reports that the Bud Light Man ("I love you, man . . . ") prefers Absolut Citron.

STINGER

The minute you open a bottle of white crème de menthe and add it to a drink, you've ventured into the spirit jungle of Stingers, Grasshoppers, and Spiders. Some are better than others, but the traditional Stinger stands tall, a superb drink at any time of the day or night, but especially pleasing as an after-dinner drink.

As with many other cocktails, the Stinger has been toyed with over the years.

Patrick Ford of New York's Wollensky's Grill says without hesitation or reservation, "Always make a Stinger dry!"

The Bar at Morton's Sean McCarthy takes exception to the Classic Stinger shown on page 170. For him, a Stinger must be shaken, never stirred. Gary Egan at Pete's Tavern agrees.

At Montreal's 737 Restaurant, Club and Lounge, barman Pierre Beaunoyer recommends using VSOP brandy instead of cognac. He says it's less expensive and tastes better.

But if you're going to make Stingers for your guests, here's the traditional way to do it.

CLASSIC STINGER

2 OZ. GOOD BRANDY
2 OZ. WHITE CRÈME DE MENTHE

Stir brandy and crème de menthe in a mixing glass with ice. Strain over ice in an old-fashioned glass. No garnish.

Note
To make a "dry" Stinger, use less white crème de menthe, perhaps a two-to-one ratio.

STINGER, MARIE MAHER

Marie Maher, that creative bartender at Windows on the World in lower Manhattan, puts her own spin on the drink.

1 1/2 OZ. BRANDY
1/2 OZ. WHITE CRÈME DE MENTHE
1/2 OZ. YELLOW CHARTREUSE

Stir brandy, crème de menthe, and chartreuse in a mixing glass with ice. Strain over ice in a cocktail glass.

RUSTY NAIL

Don't believe the adage that this drink was named by four Scottish bartenders who, when serving boorish Americans, stirred their drinks with rusty nails. Rely instead on the drink's color as having been the reason bar patrons and bartenders gave it its not terribly attractive moniker.

The Rusty Nail is a fine drink, combining two liquors that the Scots usually opt to drink straight—Scotch and Drambuie. The Drambuie gently balances the Scotch, resulting in a highly satisfying combination.

The next time you have guests to your home for a Sunday brunch, add Rusty Nails to your prebrunch drink menu, along with the traditional Bloody Marys and Screwdrivers. They set a nice tone for the food to follow.

2 OZ. SCOTCH

1 OZ. DRAMBUIE

Pour Scotch and Drambuie over ice cubes in an old-fashioned glass. Stir and serve.

THE CAPITAL GRILLE, CHICAGO

A character once asked Robert Brady to garnish his Gin and Tonic with olives.

WARD EIGHT

Unlike so many drinks whose recipes have been altered by overzealous bartenders—only occasionally for the better—the Ward Eight, synonymous with Boston and its quintessential bar, Locke-Ober, has survived the days of Prohibition unscathed.

The Ward Eight has a colorful history. In 1898 the bartender at Locke-Ober was a gent named Tom Hussion, who had many loyal followers, including a political club—the Hendricks Club (named after President Cleveland's VP, Thomas Hendricks, for no good reason)—which was controlled by Boston politician Martin Lomasney. Certain of another electoral victory that year in the city's Ward Eight, Lomasney's supporters gathered at Locke-Ober and insisted that barman Hussion whip up a special drink in honor of their leader. Hussion added a dash or two of grenadine to his basic Whiskey Sour and proclaimed it a "Ward Eight."

Ironically, Martin Lomasney was a staunch prohibitionist, and when Prohibition hit, Locke-Ober's owner reluctantly shut down, not to reopen again until the early 1950s. It's been serving its signature drink with style ever since.

CLASSIC WARD EIGHT

Here's the way it's made—always—at Locke-Ober by its skilled barman, Satcha "Dang" Hiranyaket, who's been making them the good old-fashioned way for more than ten years.

2 OZ. BLENDED WHISKEY (GENERALLY RYE)

1/2 OZ. ORANGE JUICE

1/2 OZ. FRESH LEMON JUICE

DASH OF GRENADINE

Combine all ingredients in a cocktail shaker with ice. Shake well. Strain drink into a cocktail glass.

Note

The Ward Eight is, in reality, nothing more than a Whiskey Sour with a dash of grenadine added.

LOCKE-OBER, BOSTON

Many a good bartender has had to scrape the bottom of even the celebrity barrel. But Satcha Hiranyaket of Locke-Ober, Boston, must have risen to the occasion when Supreme Court Justice David Souter stopped in for a refreshment. Had the criminal who ordered a Kahlua Sour been on the scene, there certainly would have been a judgment against him. The good judge might have had the vagabond committed to a Ward Eight in the very bar in which it was created.

OLD FASHIONED

There are those (not many) who swear by Old Fashioneds made with Scotch, or even with tequila. It's your home bar; you're free to do what you wish.

We've seen bartenders muddle the cherry right along with the other ingredients. This is anathema to Paul Mallory of Portland's Higgins Bar and Restaurant. *"Don't* muddle the cherry!" he says with conviction.

For Robert Brady, barman at Chicago's Capital Grille, the secret to making a good Old Fashioned is to pour a half ounce of whatever liquor you're using into the glass before muddling the fruit. This, he says, helps break down the fruit, resulting in a better drink.

Salvatore   Calabrese   at   The   Library   Bar   in   London's

Lanesborough Hotel likes to make his Old Fashioneds with bourbon rather than rye, and we couldn't agree with him more. After all, the drink was invented at the Pendennis Club in Louisville, Kentucky, in honor of a retired Civil War general, so the likelihood is that bourbon was the original spirit base. Salvatore also uses soda rather than water to help muddle the sugar and bitters. Perhaps it dissolves the sugar cube more rapidly.

Eddie Doyle of the Bull 'n' Finch Pub (Cheers), Boston, seconds Salvatore's selection: "Bourbon, of course."

"Muddle, muddle, muddle is the secret to a good Old Fashioned," according to Gary Egan at Pete's Tavern in New York City.

CLASSIC OLD FASHIONED

1 DASH OF ANGOSTURA BITTERS

1 SUGAR CUBE

1 TEASPOON WATER

2 OZ. RYE WHISKEY

LEMON TWIST

ORANGE SLICE AND MARASCHINO CHERRY FOR GARNISH

Muddle up the bitters, sugar, and water in an old-fashioned glass. Add the whiskey and stir. Add ice and stir again. Rim glass with a lemon twist. Garnish with an orange slice and a maraschino cherry.

Note
The original recipe calls for a cube of sugar, not granulated or refined. Also, the original recipe calls for "branch water," which is nothing more than bottled water. Any brand will do.

Old Fashioned, Marie Maher

Marie Maher at "The Greatest Bar on Earth" at Windows on the World muddles up the following in her old-fashioned glasses:

3 DASHES OF BITTERS

2 DASHES OF ORANGE JUICE

1/2 OZ. MARASCHINO CHERRY LIQUEUR

1 TEASPOON SUGAR

DASH OF WATER

1 ORANGE SLICE

2 MARASCHINO CHERRIES

3 OZ. WHISKEY

Muddle all ingredients (except whiskey) together in an old-fashioned glass. Add ice and top with whiskey.

Pat O'Brien's Bar, New Orleans

Perhaps all the oddball cocktails escaped south to New Orleans at the end of the French and Indian War. Witness a couple of favorites at Pat O'Brien's Bar:

The Simonizer: Combine ½ oz. Frangelico, ½ oz. peach schnapps, ½ oz. Chambord, and ½ oz. cream in a cocktail shaker; shake.

The Green Apple Jolly Rancher Candy: Combine ½ oz. Apple Barrel, ½ oz. melon liqueur, ½ oz. vodka, ½ oz. Collins mix, and a splash of pineapple juice in a mixing glass; stir.

Perhaps the most famous cocktail in Louisiana was invented at Pat O'Brien's—the Hurricane (page 176).

HURRICANE

This superb drink is served up at New Orleans's famed Pat O'Brien's, established in 1933 in the city's historical LaBranche Building in the French Quarter, now located on St. Peter Street. It has become so famous that the establishment has bottled Pat O'Brien's Hurricane Mix. Next time you're there, pick up a bottle for your home bar and serve your southern cousins an authentic Hurricane, using the recipe provided by barman Tony Nettleton.

4 OZ. AMBER RUM

4 OZ. PAT O'BRIEN'S HURRICANE MIX

ORANGE SLICE AND MARASCHINO CHERRY FOR GARNISH

Stir rum and mix with ice in large glass (hurricane glass). Garnish with an orange slice and a maraschino cherry.

SKYLAB

Tony Nettleton also proudly serves his customers what he calls the Skylab.

1/2 OZ. RUM

1/2 OZ. VODKA

1/2 OZ. APRICOT BRANDY

1/2 OZ. BLUE CURAÇAO

1 OZ. PINEAPPLE JUICE

1 OZ. ORANGE JUICE

ORANGE SLICE AND MARASCHINO CHERRY FOR GARNISH

Stir together all ingredients (except garnish) with ice in 14-ounce glass. Garnish with an orange slice and a maraschino cherry.

GARGOYLE

While researching *The World's Greatest Bartenders' Guide,* we not only heeded the wisdom of professional bartenders, we also sought the advice of a few friends known to run good home bars. While their approach to home bartending differs, each takes the job seriously and enjoys coming up with variations on drinks, in some cases creating his or her home bar's "signature drink."

Bard and Victoria Bloom call their home barroom "Chez Gargoyle." They do a lot of summer entertaining, serving up classic summer drinks to their guests. But they also offer their own concoction, which they call, naturally, the Gargoyle.

1 1/2 OZ. BRANDY

1 OZ. AMARETTO

4 OZ. CHILLED ORANGE JUICE

1 SCOOP ORANGE SHERBET

Blend all ingredients in blender until combined. Serve in a tall glass.

Note
Because the orange juice and sherbet are cold, there's no need for ice, unless you wish to pour the drink over cubes to prolong its coldness. Or you can throw a few cubes into the blender to make a Frozen Gargoyle.

BLUE CANOE

New York jazz musicians John Johnson and Hap Gormley enjoy creating different drinks at Johnson's home bar after playing a gig. They've come up with many original drinks, including what they call a "Blue Canoe." The ingredients sound strange, but the result is a tasty, refreshing drink.

2 OZ. VODKA

COOL BLUE RASPBERRY GATORADE

CLUB SODA

Pour vodka over ice in a tall glass. Top off with equal amounts of Gatorade and soda.

Note
Adjust ratio of Gatorade and club soda to taste.

BRONX COCKTAIL

The Bronx Cocktail has been around since the 1930s, one of many drinks that survived Prohibition and continues to be called for at our fifty greatest bars. It was named after the Bronx Zoo.

2 OZ. GIN

1/2 OZ. DRY VERMOUTH

1/2 OZ. SWEET VERMOUTH

Shake ingredients with ice in a cocktail shaker. Strain into a cocktail glass.

Variation
Many of our professional bartenders contend that an ounce of orange juice should be added in order for the drink to be an authentic Bronx Cocktail. We've enjoyed them both ways.

BROOKLYN COCKTAIL

Not to be outdone by the Bronx, bartenders in Brooklyn created their own drink: the Brooklyn Cocktail. If you decide to serve it to guests who still bemoan losing their beloved Dodgers to Los Angeles, be sure and put a bottle of the apéritif Amer Picon on your shopping list before they arrive.

2 OZ. BLENDED WHISKEY

1 OZ. DRY VERMOUTH

DASH OF MARASCHINO LIQUEUR

DASH OF AMER PICON

Shake ingredients with ice in a cocktail shaker. Strain into a cocktail glass.

METROPOLITAN

If a guest asks for a Metropolitan, you'd better ascertain which version he or she expects before going to work behind the bar. There are two distinctly different Metropolitans, each made with different ingredients.

METROPOLITAN (WITH BRANDY)

2 OZ. BRANDY

1 OZ. SWEET VERMOUTH

1 TEASPOON SUGAR

DASH OF BITTERS

Combine all ingredients in a mixing glass with ice. Stir and strain into a cocktail glass.

METROPOLITAN (WITH GIN)

2 OZ. GIN

SPLASH OF CRANBERRY JUICE

SPLASH OF MARGARITA MIX

1/2 OZ. FRESH LEMON JUICE

CRANBERRIES FOR GARNISH

Combine all ingredients in a mixing glass with ice. Stir and strain into a cocktail glass. Garnish with cranberries.

METROPOLITAN
(WITH ABSOLUT KURANT VODKA)

2 OZ. ABSOLUT KURANT VODKA

2 OZ. CRANBERRY JUICE

DASH OF FRESH LIME JUICE

1/2 OZ. SWEET-AND-SOUR MIX

LIME TWIST FOR GARNISH

Combine all ingredients (except garnish) in a cocktail shaker with ice. Stir and strain into a cocktail glass. Garnish with a lime twist.

COSMOPOLITAN

The Cosmopolitan, a cousin of the Cape Codder, is a relatively new cocktail that has a nice bite to it, thanks to the tartness of cranberry. Did the gay community of Provincetown, Cape Cod, create the Cosmopolitan? That's what we're told. Women popularized the drink, enjoying the pleasant pink color and preferring its tartness to the cloying flavor of all those syrupy sweet drinks—those "jellybean drinks"— they were told to drink in the heyday of fern bars. For that alone we owe a debt of gratitude to whoever created the Cosmopolitan.

CLASSIC COSMOPOLITAN

2 OZ. VODKA

2 OZ. CRANBERRY JUICE

1 OZ. FRESH LIME JUICE

LEMON TWIST FOR GARNISH

Combine all ingredients (except garnish) in a mixing glass with ice. Stir gently 1 to 2 seconds. Strain into a cocktail glass. Garnish with a lemon twist.

Variations

PERFECT COSMOPOLITAN

Add a dash of lemon juice.

A dash of Cointreau is also a pleasant addition to the basic taste.

COSMOPOLITAN, SEAN McCARTHY

Here's a recipe for a Cosmopolitan from Sean McCarthy, barman at The Bar at Morton's, midtown Manhattan.

2 OZ. ABSOLUT CITRON VODKA

1 OZ. COINTREAU

SPLASH OF CRANBERRY JUICE FOR COLOR

LEMON TWIST FOR GARNISH

Pour vodka, Cointreau, and cranberry juice over ice into an old-fashioned glass. Stir. Garnish with a lemon twist.

CAPE CODDER

Originally, the Cape Codder was a drink combining two ounces each of vodka and cranberry juice and a couple of teaspoons of sugar poured into a tall glass and topped off with ice water. Today's Cape Codder eschews the sugar and ice water, and sticks to the basics. Your guests from Massachusetts will love you for whipping up Cape Codders for them.

2 OZ. VODKA

5 OZ. CRANBERRY JUICE

LIME WEDGE FOR GARNISH

Combine vodka and juice in a tall glass filled with ice cubes. Stir well. Garnish with a lime wedge.

SCREWDRIVER

You would think that a mixed drink whose primary ingredient is orange juice would have been invented in Florida or, at the very least, sunny California. But its origin seems to be far from those places—in Turkey or perhaps the French Riviera. No matter. A Screwdriver is a pleasant drink and simple to make.

There have been myriad spins on the simple Screwdriver—drinks with names like Slow Comfortable Screw, Slow Comfortable Screw Up Against the Wall, Very Screwy Driver, and Creamy Screwdriver. They call for adding an ounce of Southern Comfort, tequila, or an egg yolk for the creamy version. All we can say is you'd better know your guests pretty well before you suggest, "How would you like a Slow Comfortable Screw Up Against the Wall?"

CLASSIC SCREWDRIVER

2 OZ. VODKA

5 OZ. FRESH ORANGE JUICE

Pour vodka over ice cubes in a tall glass. Add orange juice and stir.

Variations
Make a Rum Screwdriver or a Scotch Screwdriver by substituting these liquors for vodka.

PIMM'S CUP

There are those who think a Pimm's Cup is only the name of a cocktail. While a Pimm's Cup *is* a cocktail, it's also a liquor, a gin-based spirit with a fruity flavor. Well, actually, Pimm's Cup Number One is gin based. There are other Pimm's Cups with different numbers, but they're based upon spirits other than gin. Number One is the most popular, and is what's used in the Pimm's Cup Cocktail.

Pimm's Cup has been around since the mid-1800s. It's only 50 proof (25 percent alcohol), and so it goes down easily and allows you to give credence to the "Bet you can't drink just one" cliché without falling on your nose too fast.

2 OZ. PIMM'S CUP #1

SEVEN-UP SODA, LEMON SODA, OR GINGER ALE

LEMON SLICE

CUCUMBER SLICE

Pour Pimm's Cup over ice in a tall glass. Top with mixer of your choice. Squeeze juice from the lemon slice into drink and add the lemon and cucumber slices. Stir gently.

Variations

Try making Pimm's Cup with the different mixers. Each imparts a different flavor to the drink. Ginger ale is probably the mixer used in the earlier versions of the drink, so stick to that if you're a traditionalist.

BACARDI COCKTAIL

Whip up a Bacardi Cocktail without using Bacardi brand light rum, and you run the risk of a fine, imprisonment, or worse. So ruled the New York State Supreme Court back in 1936, after the Bacardi Company sued to keep bartenders from making a Bacardi Cocktail with any rum other than its own. The court decreed, "The Court finds as a clear, prepondering, and even that which would be extracted in a criminal situation, beyond a reasonable doubt, that Bacardi rum left out of a Bacardi Cocktail is not a Bacardi Cocktail, and that otherwise it is a subterfuge and fraud."

Pretty heavy stuff. Of course, Bacardi makes excellent rum, and chances are it's what you'll have proudly displayed on your back bar.

The Bacardi Cocktail was especially popular during Prohibition, a favorite of all those Americans who fled to Cuba, where no such silly rule as Prohibition had been enacted. It's a fine drink, not harsh, and pleasing to the taste buds. Actually, it's a Daiquiri with grenadine instead of sugar.

1 1/2 OZ. BACARDI LIGHT RUM

1 OZ. FRESH LIME JUICE

1 TEASPOON GRENADINE

Shake rum, lime juice, and grenadine vigorously with ice in a cocktail shaker. Strain into a cocktail glass, straight up or over ice.

KIR

A Kir is an elegant drink, whether mixed in its basic form, using dry white wine, or in its "Royale" version, with champagne rather than wine. It's a perfect drink to serve with brunch.

Laurie Wilson, writer and travel editor of *Bridal Guide* magazine, insists that the crème de cassis be poured into a large wine glass first, the wine added slowly so that the crème de cassis remains at the bottom of the drink. "That way," she says, "the drink becomes sweeter as you sip." She often adds more wine on top of the crème de cassis before finishing the drink.

And there are those who add an ounce or two of club soda to make it a longer drink.

CLASSIC KIR

5 OZ. CHILLED DRY WHITE WINE

3/4 OZ. CHILLED CRÈME DE CASSIS

LEMON TWIST FOR GARNISH

Combine wine and crème de cassis in a wine glass; stir. Garnish with a lemon twist.

KIR ROYALE

Same as a Kir, but substitute champagne for the white wine. Serve in a champagne flute.

RUSSIANS

Any drink with "Russian" in it means vodka. Armed with that knowledge, all the home bartender has to know is which other spirit to add to create the proper cocktail.

Here are the recipes of the two most popular drinks with "Russian" in their names.

WHITE RUSSIAN

2 OZ. VODKA

1 OZ. KAHLUA

1 OZ. LIGHT CREAM

Combine vodka, Kahlua, and cream in a cocktail shaker and shake well. Strain over ice in an old-fashioned glass.

BLACK RUSSIAN

2 OZ. VODKA

1 OZ. KAHLUA

Combine vodka and Kahlua in an old-fashioned glass filled with ice. Stir gently.

Note
You can see that the only differences between the white and black versions is that there is no cream in the Black Russian and that you stir a Black Russian, shake a white one.

CHOCOLATE BLACK RUSSIAN

For a sinful variation on the Black Russian, add chocolate ice cream.

1 1/2 OZ. VODKA

1 OZ. KAHLUA

2 SCOOPS CHOCOLATE ICE CREAM

Blend vodka, Kahlua, and ice cream thoroughly in a blender. Pour into a large red-wine glass.

Variation
FROZEN CHOCOLATE BLACK RUSSIAN
Add ice before blending.

J Bar, Hotel Jerome, Aspen

A "Colorado Bulldog" has been ordered there: vodka, Kahlua, cream, and Coke. General Colin Powell likes his Coke with Mount Gay Rum.

The Mayan Whore, invented at the J Bar in the 1960s, also requires Kahlua: Mix 1½ oz. tequila, 1 oz. Kahlua, 3 oz. pineapple juice, and a splash of soda, and salute the ruins—or ruination.

GODFATHER

Here's a drink none of your guests dare refuse.

2 OZ. SCOTCH

1 OZ. AMARETTO

Stir ingredients together with ice cubes in a cocktail glass.

GODMOTHER

In order to be politically correct, we must include the recipe for the Godmother.

2 OZ. VODKA

1 OZ. AMARETTO

Stir ingredients together with ice cubes in a cocktail glass.

Dubonnet Cocktail

As with the debate over the proper ratio of gin to vermouth in a Martini, the Dubonnet Cocktail engenders a similar argument. Originally, the drink called for two parts gin to one part Dubonnet. But our professional bartenders pretty much agree that the drink, in its proper form, should contain equal amounts of gin and Dubonnet. Start with that recipe and adjust according to your individual taste.

1 1/2 OZ. DUBONNET

1 1/2 OZ. GIN

DASH OF BITTERS

LEMON TWIST FOR GARNISH

Combine Dubonnet, gin, and bitters in a mixing glass with ice. Stir and strain into a cocktail glass. Garnish with a lemon twist.

Note
Many bartenders leave out the bitters.

Fuzzy Navel

The Fuzzy Navel had to wait to be created until the recent invention of peach schnapps, or peach-flavored brandy, which can be substituted for the schnapps.

2 OZ. VODKA

2 OZ. PEACH SCHNAPPS

4 OZ. ORANGE JUICE

Pour vodka, schnapps, and juice over ice in a highball glass; stir.

Variation

Salvatore Calabrese, ever the showman, shakes his Fuzzy Navel (what a sight!) and garnishes it with a slice of orange *and* a maraschino cherry. Proving that no navel can ever be *too* fuzzy.

SEX ON THE BEACH

Drinks with "Sex" in their names are designed so that the alcohol is masked by deceptively sweet additional ingredients. This makes them dangerously appealing to young drinkers. One that enjoys great popularity, due in no small part to its name, is Sex on the Beach.

2 OZ. VODKA

2 OZ. PEACH SCHNAPPS

2 OZ. ORANGE JUICE

2 OZ. CRANBERRY JUICE

Pour all ingredients over ice in a highball glass; stir.

Variation

SLEAZY SEX ON THE BEACH

Add 1 ounce Grand Marnier, but only if you're feeling particularly wasteful and have little or no respect for Grand Marnier.

THE BAR AT MORTON'S, MIDTOWN MANHATTAN

"The one unusual drink order that comes to mind," says Sean McCarthy, "is a Slow Comfortable Screw."

"Is that so totally alien to an Irishman," we asked—in jest, of course.

"Another remark like that and I'll spread the word around this place that you're a writer. See where that gets ya. A Slow Comfortable Screw is vodka, orange juice, and Galliano, with a splash of grenadine."

Reluctant to push the brawny Sean past his limit, we switched the subject to celebrities.

"Marty Springstead, head of the American League umpires, he'll have an occasional glass of white wine. Joe Namath—nonalcoholic beer. And Rodney Dangerfield will have the whole place in an uproar, then ask for a coupl'a beers to go."

HARVEY WALLBANGER

Did a surfer named Harvey drink too much vodka and Galliano at Pancho's Bar on Manhattan Beach, California, and start banging his head against a wall to give this drink its name? Or is it a creation of Galliano marketers? Drink? Fable? Both? Does it matter?

2 OZ. VODKA

4 OZ. ORANGE JUICE

1 OZ. GALLIANO

Pour vodka and orange juice over ice in a highball glass; stir. Gently "float" the Galliano on top.

Piña Colada

We've sipped this Caribbean cocktail in its place of origin, the Caribe Hilton in Puerto Rico, after catching sailfish with the legendary deep-sea angler Mike Benítez.

Salvatore Calabrese, who mixed his share of Piñas during his stint at Little Dix Bay, Virgin Gorda, suggests that you blend the ingredients for a few seconds before adding the ice, then blend again. For a more pungent rum taste, use one part dark rum and one part light rum.

2 OZ. LIGHT RUM

2 OZ. CREAM OF COCONUT

4 OZ. PINEAPPLE JUICE

MARASCHINO CHERRY AND PINEAPPLE SLICE FOR GARNISH

Blend rum, cream of coconut, and juice with ice in a blender until smooth. Pour into a goblet. Garnish with a maraschino cherry and a pineapple slice.

Variation

A few of our bartenders substitute 2 ounces of crushed pineapple for 2 ounces of the pineapple juice.

SALTY DOG

LIME WEDGE AND SALT FOR GLASS RIM
2 OZ. VODKA
4 OZ. UNSWEETENED GRAPEFRUIT JUICE

Rim a highball glass with a wedge of lime and dip it into the salt. Fill glass with ice. Pour in vodka and grapefruit juice; stir.

Variation
The nonalcoholic version of a Salty Dog is sometimes, too cutely, called a Salty Puppy. But if you want one, it would be better to tell your bartender "Let me have a Salty Dog without the vodka."

Note
Some of our professionals top off the Salty Dog with a few sprinkles of salt.

GOLDEN CADILLAC

This is an easy-to-make sweet drink that evokes fond memories of tail fins and drive-in movies.

1 OZ. CRÈME DE CACAO
3/4 OZ. GALLIANO
3/4 OZ. LIGHT CREAM

Blend crème de cacao, Galliano, and cream with ice in a blender until smooth. Pour into a wide-mouthed champagne glass.

Variation
This drink can also be made without crushed ice, and shaken.

GRASSHOPPER

The Grasshopper is in the same class of drinks as Stingers, Scorpions, Spiders, Bees, and Tarantulas. Except for the Scorpion, they're all made with either white or green crème de menthe.

Here are a couple of these recipes, beginning with the Grasshopper.

1 OZ. GREEN CRÈME DE MENTHE
1 OZ. WHITE CRÈME DE CACAO
1 OZ. LIGHT CREAM

Combine ingredients in a cocktail shaker with ice cubes. Shake vigorously. Strain into a cocktail glass.

SCORPION

2 OZ. LIGHT RUM
1/2 OZ. BRANDY
1 OZ. FRESH LEMON JUICE
2 OZ. ORANGE JUICE
1/2 OZ. ORGEAT (ALMOND) SYRUP
ORANGE SLICE AND MARASCHINO CHERRY FOR GARNISH

Blend all ingredients (except garnish) in a blender at high speed. Pour into an old-fashioned or highball glass. Garnish with an orange slice and a maraschino cherry.

SHOOTERS

Kamikaze

A Kamikaze is in a class of drinks known as "shooters." Their original recipes called for them to be served in a shot glass and downed in a single gulp. They were also conceived to make one drunk as quickly as possible. Some of these recipes have been modified to allow for sipping.

CLASSIC KAMIKAZE

2 OZ. VODKA

1 TEASPOON FRESH LIME JUICE

Stir vodka and juice with ice cubes in a mixing glass. Strain into a shot glass. Down in one motion.

Kamikaze

This recipe has been modified for sipping.

2 OZ. VODKA
1 OZ. TRIPLE SEC OR COINTREAU
2 OZ. FRESH LIME JUICE

Pour ingredients over ice in a cocktail shaker. Shake and strain over ice in an old-fashioned glass.

Ginger Kamikaze

This is another version of the Kamikaze meant for sipping.

2 OZ. GINGER VODKA
1 OZ. TRIPLE SEC
1 OZ. FRESH LIME JUICE
1 OZ. ROSE'S SWEETENED LIME JUICE
LIME WEDGE FOR GARNISH

Shake all ingredients (except garnish) vigorously with ice in a cocktail shaker. Strain into a chilled cocktail glass. Garnish with a lime wedge.

QUEEN CITY GRILL, SEATTLE

Kevin Stewart doesn't spare a thing in whipping up a pint glass full of Queen City Kamikaze or Queen City Orange Crush: Fill a pint glass with ice; add 1½ oz. vodka, a dash of Triple Sec, a splash of fresh lime juice, and a couple of lime chunks; crush it all with a long muddler stick; pour into a cocktail glass. For a Queen City Orange Crush, substitute orange juice and orange slices for lime.

NICKALASHKA

Here's a Greek shooter whose choreography is as pleasing as its taste. Peerless barman Johnny Chung, at the posh Lobby and Bar on the first floor of Hong Kong's Peninsula Hotel, recalls a German hotel guest who requested a Nickalashka about twenty years ago, but this customer asked that it be made with vodka (it can also be made with cognac) and a lemon slice covered with sugar and coffee powder.

1 ½ OZ. OUZO
1 ROUND SLICE OF LIME
SUGAR
USED COFFEE GROUNDS, OR INSTANT COFFEE IN A PINCH

Pour ouzo into a shot glass, preferably a tall one with a thin stem. Place lime slice on top of ouzo. Sprinkle sugar on one half of slice; sprinkle coffee grounds on the other half. Fold the lime slice. Suck lime juice through sugar and coffee grounds. Down ouzo in one swallow.

THE LOBBY AND BAR AT
THE PENINSULA HOTEL, HONG KONG

Jackie Chan? Two or three Piña Coladas. He has his Piñas, along with Roger Moore, who joins Sean Connery in shattering the James Bond Martini myth; Connery drinks Jack Daniel's and Coke. The Bar is most famous, though, for having been the place at which Clark Gable introduced the Screwdriver to Hong Kong.

Johnny Chung, who has worked behind the bar for thirty years, likes to serve his specialty, the Triangle: Combine equal parts of sweet vermouth, Dubonnet, Campari, and lemon juice; shake; pour over ice in a rocks glass.

Johnny also is noted for his Black Magic, Platinum Journey, and Lady Killer. Black Magic: Combine 1½ oz. dark rum, ¼ oz. apricot brandy, 5 oz. Coke, and ¼ oz. lime juice in a highball glass; stir and garnish with lime.

Platinum Journey: Combine 1½ oz. Absolut Citron, ½ oz. Tio Pepe, ½ oz. Cointreau, ½ oz. Rose's sweetened lime juice; shake well; pour into a highball glass; add 3 oz. bitter lemon; garnish with lime, lemon, and cherry.

Lady Killer: Combine 1½ oz. gin, ¼ oz. Cointreau, ¼ oz. apricot brandy, ½ oz. lemon juice, 4½ oz. pineapple juice; shake well; pour into cooler glass; garnish with orange, lemon, and cherry.

Odd, too, but popular in Hong Kong and highly recommended by the veteran barman is warm Coca-Cola. "It always sounds strange to Westerners," Johnny admits, "but it's a wonderful drink if you have a cold or a sore throat. You heat up the Coca-Cola and add slices of lemon and ginger." Is it growing on you yet? Put down the Bacardi bottle! Johnny's recipe does not call for rum.

FALLEN ANGEL

Novelist Jack Pearl, now deceased, loved his Wild Turkey bourbon. He introduced a drink, a shooter that he said was called a Fallen Angel, to one of the authors at a popular Roslyn, Long Island, bar—The Jolly Fisherman.

1 1/2 OZ. SAMBUCA
1/2 OZ. WILD TURKEY BOURBON

Fill a large shot glass three-quarters full with sambuca. Gently float the bourbon on top. Down drink in one swallow.

PETE'S TAVERN, NEW YORK

Walter Cronkite has been known to order beer with tomato juice. (The authors have witnessed Walter order an occasional cocktail aboard the QE2 in the mid-Atlantic but never a Bloody Beer. If you're going to try it, don't use ice.) Gary Egan has also served up Guinness with Coke, and whiskey with milk. We'd prefer to sit and wait for Marissa Tomei to show up and order a Wild Turkey on the rocks, followed by a Slippery Nipple (vodka and sambuca). Surely, being privy to that scene is worth the price of a drink.

SILVER SPIDER SHOOTER

Although the authors seldom order shooters, this one is a particular favorite.

½ OZ. VODKA

½ OZ. LIGHT RUM

½ OZ. TRIPLE SEC

½ OZ. WHITE CRÈME DE MENTHE

Stir all ingredients in a mixing glass with ice. Strain into a large shot glass.

ROOT BEER BARREL

Vicki Roush, at Key West's venerable Green Parrot, takes pride in serving that establishment's favorite shooter, the Root Beer Barrel. She uses a special glass for the drink—a large old-fashioned glass that flares out. Vicki claims it tastes like old-fashioned root beer candy.

ROOT BEER SCHNAPPS

BEER

Place a shot glass inside the larger old-fashioned glass. Fill the shot glass with root beer schnapps. Fill the old-fashioned glass to the brim with beer. Shoot it!

CANDIED ORANGE SLICE SHOOTER

At Atlanta's Tongue & Groove, barman Michael Harris invented the Candied Orange Slice Shooter.

1 OZ. STOLI OHRANJ VODKA

SPLASH OF GRAND MARNIER

ORANGE SLICE

SUGAR

Combine vodka and Grand Marnier and chill until very cold. Coat orange slice with sugar. Down the shot. Bite into orange slice.

COCAINE SHOOTER

Another shooter comes to us from Richard Ross of Harry's Restaurant and Bar in St. Louis. A customer ordered what he termed a "cocaine shooter," and Richard obliged, using the ingredients the customer told him to. "It was pretty good," says Richard.

1 OZ. VODKA

3/4 OZ. CHAMBORD

SPLASH OF SWEET-AND-SOUR MIX

SPLASH OF GRAPEFRUIT JUICE

Mix all ingredients with ice in a mixing glass. Strain into a shot glass. Shoot it!

TONY'S SCREAMING WEENIE

Here's an inventive shooter from Tony Nettleton, who reigns at the bar at New Orleans's Pat O'Brien's.

1/2 OZ. CURRANT VODKA

1/2 OZ. PEACH SCHNAPPS

1/2 OZ. MALIBU RUM

1/2 OZ. SOUTHERN COMFORT

1/2 OZ. AMARETTO

1/2 OZ. CRANBERRY JUICE

SPLASH OF PINEAPPLE JUICE

Mix all ingredients with ice in a mixing glass. Strain into a large shot glass. Shoot it!

COLLINS

Tom or John?

These are the two best known Collins drinks, sibling bar favorites when the weather turns sultry and the throat is parched.

What's the difference between a Tom Collins and a John Collins? Depends upon the bartender with whom you're speaking.

The original Tom Collins was made with sweet British Old Tom Gin, which might have played a part in the drink's name. Collins? Create your own legend.

The John Collins, originally made with Holland gin, probably predates the Tom Collins, although that's about as certain as the date the universe was created. These days, both the Tom and the John are often made with dry gin, except that many bartenders use gin only for the Tom Collins, and bourbon for his brother, John.

If a guest asks you for a Collins, be sure to ask, "Tom or John?" Not only will this clarify what ingredients you'll need, it also will establish you as a Collins maven. There aren't many of those around.

Here are the preferred recipes for both drinks. But like all drinks, variations abound, including substituting myriad liquors for gin and bourbon. A Collins is really nothing more than a sour with some club soda tossed in.

Tom Collins

2 OZ. GIN

1 OZ. FRESH LEMON JUICE

1 TEASPOON SUGAR

3 OZ. CLUB SODA

ORANGE SLICE AND MARASCHINO CHERRY FOR GARNISH

Shake all ingredients (except garnishes and club soda) with ice in a cocktail shaker. Strain into a collins glass with ice. Top with club soda. Garnish with an orange slice and a maraschino cherry.

Note
A collins glass is frosted. To serve a Collins in any other type of glass is blasphemy.

John Collins

2 OZ. WHISKEY (PREFERABLY BOURBON)

1 OZ. FRESH LEMON JUICE

1 TEASPOON SUGAR

3 OZ. CLUB SODA

ORANGE SLICE AND MARASCHINO CHERRY FOR GARNISH

Shake all ingredients (except garnishes and club soda) with ice in a cocktail shaker. Strain into a collins glass with ice. Top with club soda. Garnish with an orange slice and a maraschino cherry.

Note

As we've said, there are many bartenders who consider Tom and John Collins to be twins, and who make them exactly the same, using gin. If you're at someone else's home bar, or at a commercial establishment, and want a John Collins with bourbon, be specific.

Sours

The key to making any drink known as a *sour* is to achieve the perfect balance of lemon juice and sugar. After all, that's what a sour consists of—the sweetness of sugar and the tart flavor of lemon. There are sour mixers on the market that are pretty good and provide a frothy head. But your guests will appreciate the unmistakable flavor of freshly squeezed lemon juice.

The following classic recipe applies to *all* sours, whether you use whiskey, bourbon, Scotch, tequila, vodka, or brandy. We'll use whiskey since a Whiskey Sour is the most popular, followed by a Scotch Sour.

Some bartenders prefer substituting lime juice for lemon juice when making a Scotch Sour.

A dash of grenadine gives a sour a pleasant color.

THE CHINA CLUB, PARIS

Barman Justin Barbey recalls serving President Mitterand a glass of water with a cherry on a stick. He could have had a China Town, created as a tribute to Roman Polansky's *Chinatown*, in which Fay Dunaway orders a Tom Collins with mint: Combine 4 parts gin, 3 parts fresh lemon juice, and a dash of sugar in a highball glass; fill with Perrier; garnish with a branch of mint cut to look like a Bonsai tree.

Justin observes a commendable tradition of creating new and interesting cocktails to celebrate memorable occasions. When the China Club opened its downstairs jazz bar, he concocted the Sing Song: Over 5 ice cubes in a highball glass, pour 5 parts vodka; fill with grapefruit juice; top with 2 parts cherry brandy; garnish with fresh fruit.

When his second head bartender left for New Orleans to wed, Justin whipped up a batch of Deep South Sours: Combine 2 parts bourbon, 2 parts Southern Comfort, a dash of sugar, and 1 part fresh lemon juice; shake and serve straight in a cocktail glass.

To mark the China Club's entry onto the World Wide Web (chinaclub@imaginet.fr), he came up with the Spider Kiss: Combine 3 parts cognac, 2 parts Kahlua, 1 part cream; shake; serve straight in a cocktail glass; garnish with nutmeg.

WHISKEY SOUR

2 OZ. WHISKEY

1 OZ. FRESH LEMON JUICE

1 TEASPOON FINE SUGAR

ORANGE OR LEMON WEDGE AND MARASCHINO CHERRY FOR
GARNISH

Combine all ingredients (except garnishes) in cocktail shaker; shake with conviction. Strain into a sour glass. Garnish with an orange or lemon wedge and a maraschino cherry.

FIZZES

A *fizz* gets its name from the addition of club soda to various drinks in which lemon juice is also a prime ingredient. The two most famous fizzes are the Ramos Gin Fizz and the Sloe Gin Fizz, although almost any liquor can be used in a fizz.

The Ramos Gin Fizz was first enjoyed at a famous New Orleans bar owned by the Ramos Brothers. Legend has it that because the drink must be shaken long and hard, the shaker would be passed from male customer to male customer at the bar, each taking a turn until his arms gave out. A minute at high speed in a blender will do very nicely.

The classic recipe from the Ramos Brothers calls for a few ingredients our home bartenders are unlikely to have. But we felt it was of historic interest to present the way this fine drink was made in the beginning.

Classic Fizz

Makes 2 drinks.

6 OZ. DRY GIN

JUICE OF 1 LEMON

2 EGG WHITES

2 TABLESPOONS HEAVY CREAM

1 TABLESPOON SUGAR

1 TEASPOON ORANGE FLOWER WATER

CARBONATED (CHARGED) WATER

Shake . . . and shake . . . and shake with 1 cup ice in a cocktail shaker. Strain into 2 (10 oz.) glasses. Top with carbonated water.

Note

Raw eggs may contain salmonella and should never be served to anyone who is ill or has a compromised immune system.

Fizz, Danny Woo

Here's a more contemporary version of this classic drink, compliments of Danny Woo at San Francisco's elegant Compass Rose Bar in the equally elegant Westin St. Francis Hotel. While most bars do not keep orange flower water on hand, Danny Woo does, which says something about him and his bar.

1 1/4 OZ. GIN

3 DASHES ORANGE FLOWER WATER

1 OZ. SIMPLE SYRUP

12 OZ. SWEET-AND-SOUR MIX

SPLASH OF CLUB SODA

1 EGG WHITE

1 OZ. LIGHT CREAM

GRATED NUTMEG FOR GARNISH

Combine all ingredients (except nutmeg) in a blender and blend well. Pour into a highball glass. Garnish with nutmeg.

Variations
Most bartenders leave out the club soda when blending, using it to top off the drink.

A dash of Triple Sec or Cointreau spices things up for some bartenders. So does 1 ounce of lemon juice. But these creative additions are deviations from the classic approach.

Note
Raw eggs may contain salmonella and should never be served to anyone who is ill or has a compromised immune system.

SLOE GIN FIZZ

Sloe gin is nothing but gin fortified with English sloes rather than juniper berries. Sloes are the plumlike fruit of the blackthorn tree.

2 OZ. SLOE GIN

1 OZ. FRESH LEMON JUICE

1 TEASPOON FINE SUGAR

4 OZ. CLUB SODA

Shake gin, juice, and sugar well in a cocktail shaker, or blend in a blender. Pour into a highball glass with ice cubes. Top off with club soda.

MALIBU FIZZ

Kevin Bennett, who keeps things humming behind the bar of Atlanta's Martini Club, offers a recipe for a fizz that is served as a shooter.

1/2 OZ. MALIBU RUM

1/4 OZ. VODKA

1/4 OZ. GRENADINE

SPLASH OF SODA

Shake all ingredients well in a cocktail shaker. Serve in a shot glass.

COOLERS

Coolers are highballs, as opposed to cocktails. No matter what liquor you choose to use—gin, vodka, rum, brandy, tequila, or whiskey—all coolers are made the same way.

BASIC COOLER

1 TEASPOON FINE SUGAR

CLUB SODA

2 OZ. LIQUOR OF CHOICE

Dissolve sugar in 2 ounces of club soda in a tall glass. Add ice cubes. Add the liquor. Top with club soda.

Variation

Ginger ale can be substituted for club soda, and often is.

IRISH COFFEE—"GOOD MORNING, GOOD NIGHT"

We were young and impressionable when we first met the late Stanton Delaplane. We leaned together against the gunwale of a yacht in Virgin Islands waters, sipping single malt and toasting a fault-free sunset. He had a Pulitzer. We had an attitude.

"Do you really claim to have single-handedly introduced Irish Coffee to the United States of America?" we asked.

"Claim has nothing to do with it, my boy. It's documented!"

It is. Stan Delaplane, columnist for the *San Francisco Chronicle*, on the night of November 10, 1952, told Jack Koeppler, barman at San Francisco's Buena Vista (one of our fifty greatest), how to make an Irish Coffee. He had just returned from Ireland, where barman Joe Sheridan at the Shannon Airport bar had borrowed a dollop of Irish whiskey from the traditional tea, put it into American coffee, and sweetened it to accommodate his Yankee clientele. Quick as a wink, Irish Coffee! Leave it to an American scribe to spread the word.

With or without Irish Coffee, Stan Delaplane should long be remembered as a man of truth who spread many a good word. Wish we could have been there when Stan and Jack had at it, working (working?) all night to concoct the perfect Irish Coffee.

Fortunately, we *have* been there when some of the greatest Irish Coffees imaginable have been concocted on either side of the Atlantic. Take for example Joe Mahon's "Irish Coffee a la Crème." Joe, the third-generation owner of Mahon's Pub in Irvinestone, Northern Ireland, pours a measure of Bushmills Irish whiskey and a measure of Baileys Irish Cream into a heated glass (keep this heated-glass concept in mind), then tops it with coffee, two spoonfuls of sugar, and a sprinkle of chocolate. Joe is one of Ireland's foremost cocktail champions, so give this recipe serious attention.

On the opposite side of the Atlantic, Maurice O'Connell of Kennedy's, Manhattan, is no less demanding. His Irish Coffee glasses are properly heated. He suggests using a coffee liqueur, the best of Irish whiskey (it's Jamesons for Maurice), and freshly whipped cream. He likes to top his Irish Coffee off with a bit of crème de menthe.

Grayson Stover of the J Bar in Aspen's Hotel Jerome must have conspired with Maurice at one time, because their recipes mirror each other, from the Baileys to the crème de menthe.

Brian Finegold of Jardines Jazz Club, Kansas City, agrees with the need for a hot glass to start. And he says, "Always use cubed sugar; raw sugar adds a little extra body. We use heavy cream that's ice cold. Pour it into a blender with a little white crème de cacao; blend until set."

Gary Egan at Pete's Tavern in New York favors brown sugar, and he recommends floating the cream, while Kevin Stewart of Seattle's Queen City Grill (who also heats the glass) mixes the sugar and coffee together and then adds the Irish whiskey. Stewart cautions not to add too much whipped cream.

Sean McCarthy of Midtown Manhattan's Bar at Morton's favors the use of Bushmills Irish whiskey (from the oldest distillery on earth).

IRISH COFFEE, FRANK McLOUGHLIN

Another of our top fifty, Frank McLoughlin of Fado Irish Pub, Atlanta, gets real specific with his recipe:

BROWN SUGAR

6 OZ. HOT COFFEE

1 1/4 OZ. IRISH WHISKEY

FRESHLY WHIPPED CREAM

Use a 10-ounce glass, stemmed if possible. Heat the glass with hot water. Combine a spoonful of brown sugar, the coffee, and the whiskey in the warm glass and stir. Then, pouring over a spoon, float whipped cream to the top of the glass.

IRISH COFFEE, MARIE MAHER

Grandiosity, surprisingly, does not overshadow the Irish Coffee—dubbed a "Celtic Coffee"—at "The Greatest Bar on Earth" at Windows on the World. Here's its recipe, courtesy of barwoman Marie Maher:

4 1/2 OZ. HOT COFFEE

1 1/2 OZ. IRISH WHISKEY

2 OZ. FRESHLY WHIPPED CREAM

1/4 OZ. GREEN CRÈME DE MENTHE

UNSWEETENED COCOA POWDER

Add the coffee to the whiskey in a stemmed wine glass. Pour cream over the mixture on the back of a bar spoon, then pour crème de menthe over the top and dust with cocoa powder.

KELLY COFFEE

Mannix of Casa de Sierra Nevada, San Miguel de Allende, Mexico, mixes up a lot more in his concoction.

1 OZ. GRAND MARNIER

1/4 OZ. KAHLUA

1/4 OZ. BRANDY

1/4 OZ. COINTREAU

1 OZ. HOT ESPRESSO COFFEE

2 TABLESPOONS CHANTILLY CREAM

Combine all ingredients except cream in a stemmed glass and stir. Pour cream over the mixture on the back of a bar spoon.

Note
Chantilly cream is lightly sweetened whipped cream.

IRISH COFFEE, BUENA VISTA

No bar on earth, though, is as dedicated to Irish Coffee as Stan Delaplane's beloved Buena Vista. Since his visit in 1952, the Buena Vista has served more than 20 million Irish Coffees. It has its own private-label Irish whiskey.

The saloon's owners were so dedicated to the concoction that they sent a delegation to Shannon Airport to extract the original recipe from Joe

Sheridan. Back home, they solved the problem of "sinking cream" by visiting San Francisco's Mayor George Christopher. It wasn't that sinking cream was a political problem; it was that Mayor George was also a dairy farmer. He advised aging the cream for forty-eight hours and then frothing it to a fare-thee-well until it was the consistency of pancake batter.

Carrying the matter of a new drink to the sublime, we can almost picture Stan forming the Buena Vista Irish Coffee Club (which he did) and issuing membership cards (which, surely, somebody did for him).

1 TO 3 SUGAR CUBES

1 OZ. IRISH WHISKEY

STRONG BLACK COFFEE

COLD HEAVY CREAM OR WHIPPED CREAM

Heat the glass with boiling water. Add sugar to taste, whiskey, and enough coffee to fill glass about two-thirds full, and stir. Then, pouring over a spoon, float cream to the top of the glass.

Note

Cream beaten in an electric mixer takes about five seconds or stroking briskly with a fork will accomplish the same.

So whip that cream, crank up Phil Coulter on the stereo, sit back, and take a sip. *Slainte!*

CUBA LIBRE

Salvatore Calabrese likes to add the juice of one fresh lime, and that's refreshing. But we like to taste the rum in a Cuba Libre, so we end up adding the spirit, cutting down on the Coca-Cola, hedging the lime juice, and finding the definitive Cuba Libre that's right for us. It's a good recipe to play with because if you go wrong, you'll never go too far wrong, and when you get it right, you can say it's your own.

One of our greatest, Sean McCarthy of The Bar at Morton's in Midtown Manhattan, has a rule of 50/50 spirit/mixer, though we think he might make an exception with the Cuba Libre. Two ounces of Bacardi rum to six ounces of Coca-Cola is a good balance of strength and sweetness; two-to-five is perfection. Don't bother to squeeze an entire lime dry; just cut a good quarter wedge, squeeze it, and drop it in.

If you're serving it to a guy, get a heavily lipsticked woman in attendance to take a sip first, then deliver the drink with its imprint and the salutation, "Freedom reigns!"

If you're serving it to a gal, take a sip before you deliver the drink and say, "Liberty perfected!"

If you're a gal serving a Cuba Libre to a guy, you might just want to place it on a coaster in front of him and, with a wink of an eye, warn, "Fidel is watching."

AUTHENTIC CUBA LIBRE

Before we give you the "classic recipe" for this sublime rum cocktail, allow us to give you the authentic recipe—simple, pure, with no excuses—from La Bodeguita del Medio, Havana.

1 1/2 OZ. HAVANA CLUB RUM OR SUBSTITUTE

COCA-COLA

1 LIME SLICE FOR GARNISH

Pour the rum over ice in an 8-ounce glass. Fill with Coke. Stir and garnish with a lime slice.

CLASSIC CUBA LIBRE

2 OZ. RUM

5 OZ. COCA-COLA

1/4 LIME

Pour rum over ice in an 8-ounce glass. Add Coke. Squeeze the juice from the lime wedge and drop it in. Stir.

SAZERAC

The first cocktail created in America? Claiming to be the first of anything is always tricky. However, it is possible that back in the mid-1800s, all those drinks served by pretty southern belles to all those visitors arriving by train for New Orleans's Mardi Gras were in fact the first American "cocktail." They called the drink a Sazerac, after Sazerac-de-Forge, et fils Cognac, which was the main ingredient.

No one seems to know what the official recipe was, and the drink has gone through dozens of variations. Rye soon replaced cognac, and a New Orleans bartender added absinthe, which defines the Sazerac as we know it today. Except that a gentleman by the name of Antoine Amedee Peychaud substituted bitters bearing his name for the absinthe and served the drink in a French egg cup, or *coquetier*. Folks who couldn't speak French pronounced it "cock-tay"; those who overindulged called it a "cock-tail"—hence the New Orleans version of how the name was coined. The Sazerac is a splendid prebrunch cocktail. Here's how to make it:

DASH OF PERNOD

1/2 TEASPOON SUGAR

DASH OF PEYCHAUD BITTERS

1 TABLESPOON WATER

2 OZ. RYE WHISKEY

LEMON PEEL FOR GARNISH

Swirl the Pernod in a chilled cocktail glass until coated. Stir sugar, bitters, ice, and 1 tablespoon water in a mixing glass until sugar dissolves. Add whiskey and stir well. Strain into coated cocktail glass. Garnish with a lemon peel.

Variation
Substitute bourbon for rye.

POUSSE-CAFÉS

Besides being walking dictionaries of drink recipes and regular-customer preferences, and functioning as occasional lay shrinks, professional bartenders are also on stage. How they go about their craft is often visually intriguing; some have carried flamboyance to new heights of showmanship.

This is never more true than when called upon to make the challenging, often frustrating, and seemingly impossible Pousse-Café, in which colored liqueurs are layered one atop the other in a straight-sided, narrow cordial glass. It takes a steady hand; a knowledge of the specific gravity, or weight, of each of the liqueurs used; and imagination. Done right, it will dazzle your guests. But have plenty of practice under your belt before attempting a Pousse-Café. And also bear in mind that while the drink looks great, it doesn't always (usually?) taste great. But it's fun to master.

You can choose any number of liqueurs for your Pousse-Cafés. But you must know their weights relative to each other. Obviously, the first one put into the glass should be the heaviest of those you're using. The next heaviest follows. And so on. The layers don't have to be equal, but the order in which the liqueurs are poured is critical.

The liqueurs are poured slowly and carefully, actually dribbled into the glass over the back of a bar spoon, with its tip touching the side of the glass, slow and steady until the first layer is there. Then, on to layer number two, and three, and as many as you choose to add.

A tip: The same liqueur by different manufacturers won't always have the same weight, or density. In other words, you may have great success while practicing, using a certain brand of banana liqueur. But if you buy a different brand to use for guests, it may not perform the same way. So once you've mastered your own signature Pousse-Café, keep track of the brands you used and stick with them. Weights or densities are not indicated on liqueur labels, but the alcohol content is. As a rule, the higher the alcohol content, the less weight the liqueur will have.

Here are a few Pousse-Cafés you might want to try.

POUSSE-CAFÉ

The amount of each you pour is up to you, although the standard is generally ½ ounce of each.

GRENADINE

YELLOW CHARTREUSE

CRÈME DE CASSIS

WHITE CRÈME DE MENTHE

GREEN CHARTREUSE

BRANDY

Ingredients are listed in the order they should be poured into a straight-sided, narrow cordial glass. Pour grenadine slowly and carefully, almost a drop at a time, over the back of a bar spoon, with its tip touching the side of the glass. Repeat with remaining layers.

SMALL POUSSE-CAFÉ

CRÈME DE CACAO

APRICOT BRANDY

LIGHT CREAM

Ingredients are listed in the order they should be poured into a straight-sided, narrow cordial glass. Pour crème de cacao slowly and carefully, almost a drop at a time, over the back of a bar spoon, with its tip touching the side of the glass. Repeat with remaining layers.

ARTISTIC POUSSE-CAFÉ

Here's a more ambitious Pousse-Café in which colors are combined to create a pretty drink for your artistic guests.

GRENADINE

GREEN CRÈME DE MENTHE

PARFAIT AMOUR

GALLIANO

BLACK SAMBUCA

Ingredients are listed in the order they should be poured into a straight-sided, narrow cordial glass. Pour grenadine slowly and carefully, almost a drop at a time, over the back of a bar spoon, with its tip touching the side of the glass. Repeat with remaining layers.

Variation

Create your own Pousse-Cafés, determining the order in which the liqueurs should be poured based upon their densities relative to their alcohol content: The higher the alcohol content, the "lighter" the liquor.

RED, WHITE, AND BLUE POUSSE-CAFÉ

If you're having a patriotic Fourth-of-July party, you might want to serve a Red, White, and Blue Pousse-Café. Because only three liqueurs are used, use more of each, perhaps a full ounce or even 1½ ounces.

GRENADINE

PEACH SCHNAPPS

BLUE CURAÇAO

Ingredients are listed in the order they should be poured into a straight-sided, narrow cordial glass. Pour grenadine slowly and carefully, almost a drop at a time, over the back of a bar spoon, with its tip touching the side of the glass. Repeat with remaining layers.

ANGEL'S KISS

A popular Pousse-Café called an "Angel's Kiss":

CRÈME DE CACAO

PRUNELLE

CRÈME DE VIOLETTE

LIGHT CREAM

Ingredients are listed in the order they should be poured into a straight-sided, narrow cordial glass. Pour crème de cacao slowly and carefully, almost a drop at a time, over the back of a bar spoon, with its tip touching the side of the glass. Repeat with remaining layers.

ANGEL'S DELIGHT

GRENADINE

TRIPLE SEC

CRÈME YVETTE

LIGHT CREAM

Ingredients are listed in the order they should be poured into a straight-sided, narrow cordial glass. Pour grenadine slowly and carefully, almost a drop at a time, over the back of a bar spoon, with its tip touching the side of the glass. Repeat with remaining layers.

MAHON'S PUB, IRVINESTONE, NORTHERN IRELAND

A lady won the all-Ireland cocktail contest for her creator, owner Joe Mahon. She's called the Scarlet Lady, and here are her dimensions: 2 parts vodka, 4 parts cherry brandy, 4 parts Tia Maria; shake; serve straight; pour cream on top.

After winning the Bartender Association of Ireland's contest with the Scarlet Lady in 1983 (the first-ever winner outside Dublin), Joe did it again in 1987 with the Mist of Eire, which replicates the colors of the Irish flag—green, white, and gold: 4 parts Midori melon liqueur, 3 parts crème de banane, 3 parts vodka, fresh orange juice; shake; pour cream on top; garnish with nutmeg.

When Joe's clientele concoct their own libations, it can get downright weird. One fellow orders a large Dewars and a Gin and Tonic and drinks them simultaneously. A popular drink at the bar is brandy and milk. And there are those who mix black currant into their Guinness.

PUNCHES

Punches should be ladled into lowball glasses from a large glass punch bowl in which floats a block of ice. Punch is the mixologist's answer to the casserole. You can mix it all up in advance without anybody watching, then plop it in the middle of the table and tell all your guests to help themselves.

Punches go back as far as the seventeenth century, when the British, flush with success after capturing the rum-soaked island of Jamaica from Spain, introduced the concept of mixing rum with lots of other ingredients. It caught on in the British Isles, so much so that families routinely drank rum-laced punch with dinner.

The origins of the term *punch* are unclear. A "puncheon" is an oversized wine cask that holds more than one hundred gallons. Then there is the Hindu word *panch*, meaning "five"; most punches are made with five or more ingredients.

Here are some classic punches, and some that are just plain fun.

EGGNOG

Makes about 40 servings.

12 EGGS, SEPARATED
2 CUPS CONFECTIONERS' SUGAR
1 PINT COGNAC
1 PINT LIGHT RUM
6 CUPS MILK
1 PINT (2 CUPS) HEAVY CREAM
FRESHLY GRATED NUTMEG

Beat the egg yolks and sugar together until thick, then slowly stir in the cognac, rum, milk, and cream. Cover and refrigerate until cold. Refrigerate egg whites separately.

About 15 minutes before serving, remove egg whites from refrigerator to warm slightly. Beat egg whites until stiff but not dry and fold into the chilled mix, but don't stir. Sprinkle with some nutmeg and serve.

Note
Raw eggs may contain salmonella and should never be served to anyone who is ill or has a compromised immune system.

Hot Mulled Wine

Makes about 12 servings.

In late November, when your favorite football team is on a sure-to-win, ball-control drive that seems to be taking forever and you want to stay, but the damp wind creeping up the sleeves of your coat is nudging you to leave, pour yourself a bracing mug of Hot Mulled Wine. The home team will be glad you did.

2 CUPS BOTTLED WATER

2 WHOLE CINNAMON STICKS

¹/₄ CUP SUGAR SYRUP

2 (750 ML) BOTTLES RED WINE, SUCH AS CONCHA Y TORO
CABERNET

4 OZ. COGNAC

LEMON TWISTS

Bring water, cinnamon, and syrup to a boil in a large nonreactive pan; add the wine and heat slowly until hot. Stir in the cognac and remove from heat. Add lemon twists.

Claret Cup

A wine-based punch on the cooler side, Claret Cup can be used to toast your winners but should not be abused to curse your losers. This can be served with filet mignon or pizza. You don't need to join the horsy set to mix it. Just read on.

1 TABLESPOON SUGAR

1 LITER CHILLED CLUB SODA

2 (750 ML) BOTTLES CHILLED RED WINE, SUCH AS

VENDANGE CABERNET

1/2 CUP TRIPLE SEC

1/2 CUP WATER

1/4 CUP PORT

JUICE OF 1 LEMON

ORANGE SLICES FOR GARNISH

Mix sugar with 1 cup of the club soda in a saucepan while heating over medium heat. Cool to room temperature. Combine remaining ingredients except orange slices and remaining club soda in a large punch bowl and stir vigorously. Refrigerate until chilled. Stir in remaining cold club soda. Garnish with orange slices.

HOT APPLE RUM PUNCH

Take off with your favorite hiking partner into the autumnal woods. Wear yourselves out. Get back to the cabin (apartment) a moment before her (him), so that you can shake and throw the ingredients into a pot and heat them up on the stove. Stall awhile, telling her (him) how the brisk hike and exercise has ruddied her (his) cheeks and has made her (him) particularly sexy looking. Check your watch. By now—if you've got a good line—everything should be coming to a boil. Time to relax, shed that anorak and those hiking boots, crank up the fire, sip some Hot Apple Rum Punch, and mellow.

1 LITER BARBANCOURT RUM

1 QUART FRESH APPLE CIDER

A FEW CRUMBLED CINNAMON STICKS

3 TABLESPOONS BUTTER

Combine all ingredients in a large nonreactive pan over medium heat. Simmer about 20 minutes to blend flavors. Serve hot.

SANGRIA

Makes about 30 servings.

Olé! Oh well. Some folks still drink this stuff. And it's always fun for a theme party. This is one time that the inexpensive brands work great. Here's how to make it:

2 (750 ML) BOTTLES RED WINE

1 (750 ML) BOTTLE CHAMPAGNE

6 OZ. BRANDY

6 OZ. VODKA

4 OZ. FRESH LEMON JUICE

4 OZ. ORANGE JUICE

2 TABLESPOONS SUGAR

ICE RING

1 TO 2 ORANGES, SLICED CROSSWISE

Combine wine, champagne, brandy, vodka, juices, and sugar in a punch bowl with ice cubes and stir. Add the ice ring and orange slices.

FRUIT PUNCH

With a sultry sun setting behind your crowded patio, there may be nothing more refreshing than a not-too-sweet Fruit Punch. This should be ladled, and there's nothing wrong with slipping some ice into the guests' glasses.

Creating original punches, as with concocting signature cocktails, is a pleasant activity that can help establish your reputation as the "summer hostess with the mostest." Experiment with ingredients such as Cointreau, apple juice, nutmeg, bitters, maple syrup, Calvados, walnut or pecan liqueurs, cream of coconut, cider, cinnamon, and coffee.

Some basic tips:

- Add any ingredient that bubbles last.
- Also add ice last, and make it a large block (see section on using ice (page 82).
- Avoid using ice in the punch itself by placing the punch bowl in a larger vessel packed with crushed ice.
- Punches are meant to be festive presentations. Use your fanciest punch bowl (or a friend's), and be creative in decorating the table surrounding it.

BASIC FRUIT PUNCH

1 LITER VODKA, SUCH AS RED CROWN OR EQUIVALENT

1 (750 ML) BOTTLE WHITE WINE, SUCH AS AN INEXPENSIVE
PINOT GRIGIO

2 (12 OZ.) CANS FROZEN PINEAPPLE JUICE CONCENTRATE

1 LITER CHILLED SODA WATER

Mix everything together except the soda water. Refrigerate until chilled. Stir in the soda water, and serve.

THE BAR AT THE HOTEL BEL-AIR, LOS ANGELES

Less exotic, but gaggingly wasteful, is the Louis XIII Cognac (at $95 per ounce) ordered with Coke. Not to worry; it was not French President Jacques Chirac who caused Barman Don Mills to commit such a travesty. The President and his First Lady liked Don's Planters Punch so well they'd take it with them to the airport.

We recommend Don's Pink Swan: equal measures of Bacardi añejo rum, Cointreau, sweet-and-sour mix, and 2 maraschino cherries; blend; pour into a cocktail glass rimmed with sugar; garnish with a lime slice, cherry, and short straw.

SPECIAL TROPICAL DRINKS

Because our two professional bartenders in the Caribbean—Neil Felix of Spicers Bar at the Rex Grenadian Hotel in Grenada and Luciano "Magic" Pilar of the Extasis Bar, Sinner's Bar and Pool Bar, AMHSA Paradise Beach Club & Casino, the Dominican Republic—provided so many wonderful original and creative tropical drinks, we felt it only appropriate to devote a special section to them.

Tropical drinks are fertile ground for experimentation. Generally, such drinks involve a number of ingredients: The entire world of spices, herbs, mixers, and a wide variety of liquors and liqueurs are at the bartender's disposal. These two gentlemen take great pride in concocting new and satisfying drinks using the widest of palates—a touch more of this, an extra dash of that.

But it isn't just a matter of blind experimentation. Anyone who's spent time in the Caribbean knows that the best bartenders there have a keen sense of what ingredients are likely to go with each other, which liquor will be enhanced by which fruit, what mixer will blend perfectly with each different combination. No surprise that they tend to use ingredients readily available in their countries. In a few cases, you probably won't be able to duplicate some of these drinks, but a little creative imagination will go a long way.

The authors urge you to create your own tropical masterpieces. In the meantime, here are a number of award-winning drinks, created by our two professional Caribbean barmen, guaranteed to please your hot-weather guests.

Note
We flipped a coin to decide which of these two gentlemen's recipes will come first. That was for our own convenience. They're both winners in the world of bartending. We should also mention that formal competition among bartenders is a way of life and a source of great satisfaction in the tropics. The chief beneficiaries of such activity are, of course, the guests at their respective hotels.

Here are recipes from Luciano Pilar of Extasis Bar, Sinner's Bar and Pool Bar, the Dominican Republic:

BANANA MAMA COCKTAIL
(FIRST PRIZE, 1991)

1 1/4 OZ. WHITE RUM

3/4 OZ. CREAM OF COCONUT

1 1/2 OZ. PINEAPPLE JUICE

1/2 OF A BANANA

Blend all ingredients with ice in a blender. Serve frozen.

COCKTAIL DULCE MARÍA
(SWEET MARY)

1 OZ. VODKA

1/2 OZ. AMARETTO

2 OZ. PINEAPPLE JUICE

1 OZ. ORANGE JUICE

Shake all ingredients in a cocktail shaker with ice. Strain over ice in a highball glass.

DELICIA

1 OZ. GIN

2 OZ. ORANGE JUICE

1/2 OZ. PEACH LIQUEUR

Stir all ingredients with ice in a mixing glass. Strain into a wide champagne glass.

CRAZY MOON

1/2 OZ. BOURBON
1/2 OZ. CREAM OF COCONUT
2 OZ. PINEAPPLE JUICE
1/2 OZ. PASSION FRUIT JUICE

Shake all ingredients in a cocktail shaker with ice. Strain into a highball glass.

SONRISA (SMILE)

1 OZ. BLENDED WHISKEY
1/2 OZ. TRIPLE SEC

Shake all ingredients in a cocktail shaker with ice. Strain into a highball glass.

PARADISE

1 OZ. DARK RUM

1/2 OZ. AMARETTO

1/2 OZ. TRIPLE SEC

2 OZ. ORANGE JUICE

DASH OF GRENADINE

1 OZ. FRESH LEMON JUICE

Shake all ingredients in a cocktail shaker with ice. Serve in a tall glass.

FRESCA PRIMAVERA (FRESH SPRING)

1 OZ. BRANDY

1/2 OZ. GREEN CRÈME DE MENTHE

1/2 OZ. FRESH LEMON JUICE

Shake all ingredients in a cocktail shaker with ice. Serve in a cocktail glass.

Dominican Sunrise

1 OZ. TEQUILA

1/2 OZ. SUGAR SYRUP

2 OZ. FRESH LEMON JUICE

2 DROPS OF GRENADINE

Shake all ingredients except grenadine in a cocktail shaker with ice. Serve in a cocktail glass. Add grenadine.

Merengue

1 OZ. DARK RUM

1/2 OZ. CRÈME DE CACAO

1/2 OZ. SWEET VERMOUTH

3 OZ. ORANGE JUICE

Blend all ingredients with ice in a blender. Serve frozen in a highball glass.

FIESTA

1 OZ. WHITE RUM
1 OZ. PINEAPPLE JUICE
2 OZ. ORANGE JUICE
1/2 OF A BANANA

Blend all ingredients with ice in a blender. Serve frozen in a cocktail glass.

PASSION

EQUAL AMOUNTS OF BEER AND CAMPARI

Combine beer and Campari in an old-fashioned glass. Stir gently.

MANGUITO RICO
(FOURTH PLACE, 1993)

1 OZ. VODKA
1/2 OZ. COINTREAU
2 OZ. MANGO JUICE

Shake all ingredients in a cocktail shaker with ice. Serve in a cocktail glass.

ANDROMEDA
(FIRST PRIZE, 1995)

1/4 OF A BANANA

1/4 OZ. TRIPLE SEC

1/4 OZ. AMARETTO

2 OZ. ORANGE JUICE

DASH OF GRENADINE

ORANGE TWIST FOR GARNISH

Shake all ingredients (except garnish) in a cocktail shaker with ice. Serve in a large cup. Garnish with an orange twist.

CONDESA DESCALZA
(THIRD PLACE, 1994)

1 OZ. WHITE RUM

1/4 OZ. DRY VERMOUTH

2 OZ. GUANABANA JUICE

1/2 OZ. PARFAIT AMOUR

Blend all ingredients with ice in a blender. Serve frozen in a cocktail glass.

TAINO
(THIRD PLACE, 1997)

1 OZ. DARK RUM

1/2 OZ. GIN

2 OZ. TAMARIND JUICE

1 OZ. SYRUP SUGAR

Shake all ingredients in a cocktail shaker with ice. Serve over ice in a highball glass.

Now for equally inventive and delicious tropical drinks from Neil Felix of Spicers Bar, Grenada, who won the 1997 Caribbean "Battle of the Bartenders."

CARIBBEAN SENSATION

1 OZ. WHITE RUM

1 OZ. DARK RUM

2 OZ. PINEAPPLE JUICE

1 OZ. BLUE CURAÇAO

2 OZ. CREAM OF COCONUT

GRAPEFRUIT OR ORANGE WEDGE FOR GARNISH

Blend all ingredients (except garnish) with ice in a blender for 1 second. Serve in a cocktail glass. Garnish with a grapefruit or an orange wedge.

Scorpion

1 3/4 OZ. LIGHT RUM

1/2 OZ. BRANDY

1 BANANA

2 OZ. MILK

2 OZ. CREAM OF COCONUT

MARASCHINO CHERRY AND BANANA SLICE

FOR GARNISH

Blend all ingredients (except garnishes) with ice in a blender for 30 seconds. Serve in a cocktail glass. Garnish with a maraschino cherry and banana slice.

Banana Quit

1 1/4 OZ. IRISH CREAM

2 OZ. CREAM OF COCONUT

2 OZ. EVAPORATED MILK

1/2 OF A RIPE BANANA

PINEAPPLE SLICE, BANANA SLICE, AND MARASCHINO

CHERRY FOR GARNISH

Blend all ingredients (except garnishes) with ice in a blender for 30 seconds. Serve in a cocktail glass. Garnish with pineapple, banana, and maraschino cherry.

BANANA KOW

3 OZ. GROUND NUTMEG

3 OZ. WATER

1 1/2 OZ. WHITE RUM

1 OZ. MILK

2 OZ. CREAM OF COCONUT

1/2 OF A RIPE BANANA

PINEAPPLE SLICE AND MARASCHINO CHERRY FOR GARNISH

GRATED NUTMEG FOR GARNISH

Boil nutmeg and water until syrupy. Blend remaining ingredients (except garnishes) with ice in a blender for 30 seconds. Serve in a cocktail glass. Garnish with pineapple and maraschino cherry, and sprinkle with nutmeg.

RUM PUNCH

1 OZ. WHITE RUM

1/2 OZ. DARK RUM

1/2 OZ. FRESH LIME JUICE

1 OZ. PINEAPPLE JUICE

2 DASHES OF ANGOSTURA BITTERS

1/2 OZ. PINEAPPLE SYRUP

MARASCHINO CHERRY AND GRATED NUTMEG FOR GARNISH

Shake all ingredients (except garnishes) in a cocktail shaker with ice. Serve in a cocktail glass. Garnish with a maraschino cherry and a sprinkle of nutmeg.

Note
All recipes in this tropical drink section can be topped off with a tiny parasol, and often are by these bartenders. Your choice.

SPICERS BAR IN ST. GEORGES, GRENADA

During his visit, did the Prime Minister of Canada order a cool, tropical drink like barman Neil Felix's Brown Skin Girl? Are we digressing? Not at all. Here's the recipe: 1½ oz. vodka, ½ oz. amaretto, ½ oz. Kahlua, 2 oz. cream of coconut; whip with crushed ice in a blender for 1 second. Garnish with a sprinkle of cinnamon, a wedge of stripped orange, a cherry, and a parasol.

WOLLENSKY'S GRILL, MANHATTAN

Weirdest drink? "Nelson's Blood—half cognac, half port . . . "

"Not Louis XIII . . ."

"No, not that bad."

"Who ordered it, Billy Martin?"

"No. Billy liked his Old Grand-Dad Manhattans."

"How about Jackie O'?"

"Ginger ale with a twist."

"What do you recommend?"

"Vodka Sonic: one part vodka, one part soda, one part tonic, wedge of lime."

"Thanks, Pat."

"Hey, wait a minute. Don't you want to know what Gordie Howe drinks?"

"Molson ale."

"How'd ya know?"

"He was a hockey player."

"Right. What are you going to have to eat?"

"Caesar salad."

RAY'S BOATHOUSE, SEATTLE

Patrick Negron once had a lady step up to his bar and ask for a Caesar salad. But she said it kind of funny.

"Her jaw was wired shut and she was forced to drink everything," Patrick reports. "As a result, I made a blended Caesar salad with croutons and all, and a blended order of hummus, including the pita bread. I made it, and she drank it. It was tough to watch."

One local gent purchased his sailing yacht in New Zealand. It figures that, despite the fact that Ray's Boathouse carries nineteen local microbrews, the sailor only orders Steinlager beer.

"We carry Steinlager specifically for this gentleman," Patrick reports.

When we were young, we thought the corner bar carried Budweiser specifically for us.

Patrick's Yellow Bird is popular with locals: equal parts vodka, rum, orange juice, banana liqueur, and Galliano.

THE CAPITAL BAR, LITTLE ROCK

Did President Clinton ever sit at the bar? Want to know who was with him? Could have been any of the following: John Ritter, Andy Rooney, Ed Bradley, Ron Howard, Burt Reynolds, Jerry Van Dyke, Tom Bosley, Sinbad, Scotty Pippen, Charles Barkley, James Worthy, Gregory Hines, Paula Poundstone, Kevin Bacon, Luther Vandross, Tony Dorset, Sean Penn, Leslie Nielson, Kevin Greene, or Sidney Moncrief, to name a few. Who says this isn't a president of the common folk?

Can you just imagine being barman Khalil Moussa and having to deal with all those raging egos? Surely Charles Barkley and Andy Rooney were never there at the same time, or the caustic commentator might still be picking plate glass out of his scalp.

Strange requests include cognac neat, with a Coke chaser. Others have savored XO with their Coke, milk with their bourbon, and bourbon with their cranberry juice.

Surely Khalil would have preferred to have devoted his time to his labor-intensive Cafe Ashley's: 1¼ oz. brandy, orange peel, brown sugar, nutmeg, cinnamon, ¾ oz. Kahlua, ¾ oz. Grand Marnier, lemon peel, coffee or espresso, and whipped cream. Heat the brandy; pour it over the orange peel; add brown sugar, nutmeg, and cinnamon; dissolve well. Add Kahlua, Grand Marnier, and lemon peel; pour coffee or espresso over the top; garnish with whipped cream.

Another Capital Bar original is the Irish Quaalude: 1 oz. Irish whiskey (Jamesons), 1 oz. Baileys Irish Cream, 1 oz. Frangelico. Serve chilled over ice or straight up. His Shady Lady: 1½ oz. Beefeater gin, 2 oz. orange juice, 2 oz. cranberry juice, 1 oz. grenadine. Serve chilled over ice, garnished with a lime slice and a maraschino cherry.

APPENDIX

Answers to Our Questionnaire

Besides providing the authors, and our readers, with advice on making perfect drinks, our professional bartenders were asked:

- What are the most unusual drink requests you've received?
- What have celebrities ordered at your bars?
- What drives you nuts as a bartender?
- What sort of customer pleases you most?

Some bartenders declined to identify celebrity drink orders, citing confidentiality, but most didn't hesitate. The replies to the questions about "good" and "bad" customers were fairly consistent, and we offer their responses in the form of a survey result.

UNUSUAL DRINK REQUESTS AND CELEBRITY DRINK ORDERS

The unusual drink requests and celebrity drink orders, as reported by our professional bartenders at the world's greatest bars, can be found in the shaded boxes distributed throughout the recipe chapter. Also, some of the bartenders' more unusual drink recipes are also included in the boxes.

While it certainly isn't necessary for the home bartender to be prepared for such outlandish requests, it might be fun to be ready for one or two. And, even if these drinks are never ordered, they make for some easy cocktail party conversation.

MOST ANNOYING CUSTOMERS

Here's what our bartenders said when asked about customers who drive them nuts. The numbers indicate how many gave that response.

10   Customers who get drunk

8   Customers who don't know what they want

8   Those who don't tip, or tip small

4   Customers who rudely try to get my attention (clapping hands, snapping fingers, etc.)

4   Those who are just plain rude and ill-mannered

4   Customers who think they know more about making drinks than I do

3   Ordering coffee or tea in a bar

3   Customers who are never satisfied

3   Deliberately ordering an obscure drink to test me

3   Customers who don't respect me as a professional

2   Impatient customers

1   Those who want me to pour bigger drinks

1   Someone who wants to dominate my time

1   Morose customers

1   Customers who ask me, "Do you make a good . . . ?"

1   Customers who don't heed the "Fasten Seatbelt" sign and return to their seats (obviously the bartender on Virgin Atlantic's 747s)

Most Appreciated Customers

Now for their answers to which types of customers please them the most. The numbers indicate how many gave that response.

17   People who are basically happy and upbeat

10   Customers who respect me as a professional

5   Those who know what drinks they like and want

3   Customers who know their limit

3   Customers who are willing to try a new drink

1   Pleasant eccentrics who liven up a bar

1   Customers who are celebrating something

1   Customers who are there in my bar (the quintessential political bartender)

INDEX

Drink recipe titles and types of liquor are in roman type; informational entries are in italic. Drinks are also grouped according to type of liquor/liqueur (in bold) that is used in making them.